Battles & Sieges of the Peninsular War

GW00671422

Battles & Sieges of
the Peninsular War

Corunna, Busaco, Albuera,
Ciudad Rodrigo, Badajos,
Salamanca, San Sebastian & Others

W. H. Fitchett

LEONAUR

Battles & Sieges of the Peninsular War: Corunna, Busaco, Albuera,
Ciudad Rodrigo, Badajos, Salamanca, San Sebastian & Others
by W. H. Fitchett

Published by Leonaur Ltd

ISBN: 978-1-84677-308-2 (hardcover)
ISBN: 978-1-84677-307-5 (softcover)

http://www.leonaur.com

Publisher's Note

The opinions expressed in this book are those of the author
and are not necessarily those of the publisher.

Contents

Publisher's Note

The Peninsular War was a prolonged conflict in which an alliance of Great Britain, Spain and Portugal fought against France on the Iberian Peninsula during the Napoleonic Wars. The war was caused by the invasion of Spain by Napoleon's French armies in 1808 and lasted until the Sixth Coalition defeated Napoleon in 1814.

The Spanish struggle against the French was, with the help of her allies, a war in which set-piece battles between huge armies and conventional siege warfare, worked hand in hand with guerrilla warfare as the hatred of the French by the Spanish people led to the formation of highly effective mountain fighting units made up of ordinary people, partisans, rather than trained soldiers. The success of the Spanish struggle for freedom was in part decided by the exploits of the guerrilla bands and the inability of Napoleon Bonaparte's large armies to pacify the people of Spain. French units in Spain, forced to guard their vulnerable supply lines, were constantly in danger of being cut off and overwhelmed by the partisans, and proved themselves unable to ultimately defeat the allied armies.

In the final years of war, with France gravely weakened, the allied army, commanded by Sir Arthur Wellesley, fought across Spain from Portugal and pursued a series of offensives that forced the French back across the Pyrenees and liberated Spain.

This book concentrates on the activities of the British Army in this famous war—particularly upon the campaigns fought under the leadership of Wellesley, later the Duke of Wellington. Here are victories, defeats, retreats, sieges and assaults—all fought under the blazing Spanish sun or in the freezing cold of mountain passes.

CHAPTER 1

Corunna

"As to the English armies, I will chase them from the Peninsula!" Into that sentence, spoken to a great assemblage of the notables of Spain at Charmartin, Napoleon compressed the wrathful purpose which led to the fierce, swift, sure, and bloody campaign ended at Corunna.

It may be admitted that, at that particular moment, Napoleon had good reasons for turning in warlike wrath upon the British. Some two months before, in a proclamation to his armies, Napoleon wrote: "Soldiers, I have need of you. The hideous presence of the leopard contaminates the Peninsula of Spain and Portugal. In terror he must fly before you. Let us bear our triumphal eagles to the pillars of Hercules!" In an address, too, published in the *Moniteur* of October 26, 1808, Napoleon wrote: "In a few days I shall set out to place myself at the head of my army; shall crown at Madrid the King of Spain, and plant my eagles on the towers of Lisbon."

Napoleon, in a word, was determined to grasp "the Spanish nettle." French arms had not prospered in the Peninsula. The Emperor's marshals were in nominal possession of the country; but one French force had been beaten, and had surrendered at Baylen; and Vimieiro, won by British bayonets, had driven the French eagles out of Portugal.

Napoleon, taking advantage of the pause in the great wars of the Continent, which followed the conference at Erfurt, determined to overthrow all opposition in the Peninsula, as with the stroke of a thunderbolt.

Some 70,000 Spanish soldiers were in arms against him. But they were scattered along the line of the Ebro, over a distance of 200 miles, and under three independent commanders. They were badly armed and worse drilled. Their generals had no warlike knowledge, and hated each other almost more than they hated the French. Wild ravines and swift and bridgeless rivers broke these forces up into disconnected fragments. Napoleon himself years afterwards, at St. Helena, in a spasm of bitter frankness, said, "The Spanish ulcer destroyed me;" and British statesmen, in some dim, blundering fashion, realising what an entanglement Spain might prove to Napoleon, had begun to feed the war in Spain. But their methods were of almost incredible stupidity. In the early days of November 1808, there were 30,000 British troops in Spain; but they were broken up into three independent divisions, separated by nearly a hundred miles from each other, without any common base, and in touch neither with each other nor with the Spanish armies. The three British divisions, in brief, and the three Spanish armies not 100,000 strong taken altogether were scattered, like fragments from some exploded planet, across the north of Spain, from the Asturian mountains to Saragossa. No one brain shaped their plans; no single will controlled them.

And upon this military chain, of which each link was already broken, Napoleon suddenly poured, like a tempest, the whole warlike strength of France. All through the month of October he was hurrying through the wet passes of the Eastern and Western Pyrenees his choicest troops, the fierce warriors who had struck down one after another the great Powers of the Continent, the veterans of Jena and Austerlitz and Friedland. The eight corps which formed the army now flowing like a deluge through the Pyrenees were under the command of generals into the syllables of whose very names the echoes of a hundred victories were packed: Soult and Lannes, Mortier and Ney, St. Cyr and Bessieres. And the fiercest and most splendid intellect ever employed in the service of war since the days of Hannibal that of Napoleon himself governed the whole movement. For nearly four weeks the road from Bayonne to Vittoria was crowded with infantry and cavalry and guns. The Imperial Guard itself, with the halo of a hundred victories on its bayonets, formed part of the great host pouring southward into Spain.

As the French forces deployed from the passes they formed a mighty host more than 300,000 strong, of whom 40,000 were cavalry, while in equipment, in discipline, in martial ardour, in that gay and reckless valour which is the note of the French character, they formed one of the most terrible fighting instruments known to history.

There is no space to describe here the sudden and terrible fashion in which the tempestuous strategy of Napoleon struck down the Spanish forces. Napoleon swept over them, in fact, with something of the breathless speed and resistless fury of a tropical whirlwind. The Emperor reached Bayonne on November 3; within three weeks three Spanish armies were not so much overthrown as annihilated. They had been smitten at Espinosa, at Burgos, at Tudela; and scattered fugitives, without artillery, supplies, or ammunition, had taken refuge in the rugged mountains at the head-waters of the Ebro, or amongst the Guadarrama Hills, or behind the walls of Saragossa. On December 2 the cavalry of the French Guard were gathered like a threatening cloud on the hills which overlook Madrid from the northwest; and on December 4 the French eagles flew over Retiro, and Madrid was captured!

Spain lay, in a word, at Napoleon's mercy. His cavalry could swoop, almost without check, over the fertile southern provinces. On December 20 the sixth corps under Ney, the Imperial Guard, and the reserve, under the personal command of Napoleon, stood ready to begin that great triumphant march to the south-west, which was to end at Lisbon. The Imperial muster-roll showed at that moment that the French forces in Spain numbered more than 330,000 men, with 60,000 horses and 400 guns; and Spain was, in Sir John Moore's terse phrase, "without generals, without armies, without a government." What human force could arrest a strategy framed by what Napier calls "the mightiest genius of two thousand years," and carried out by more than 300,000 of the finest soldiers of that period, with a glow of victory in their very blood?

It is a matter of sober history that the daring resolve of a single British soldier arrested the whole of Napoleon's designs, diverted the march of all his mighty and crowded battalions, and, in the darkest hour of its fortunes, saved Spain! "I will sweep the English armies from the Peninsula," said Napoleon, as, from under the walls of Madrid, he set out on what he meant to be the swiftest and most dazzling campaign of his life. Terrible is the irony of history! As a matter of fact, the British armies chased the French from the Peninsula, and in turn poured through the passes of the Pyrenees on France; and defeat in Spain finally overthrew Napoleon's throne. "It was the Spanish

ulcer," as he himself said in wrathful anguish, "that destroyed me." But there would have been no 'Spanish ulcer' there might have been no storming of Badajos, no Vittoria, no Salamanca, and perhaps no Waterloo and no St. Helena if, at the moment when Napoleon was about to set out on his march to Lisbon at the head of what seemed resistless forces, Sir John Moore, with 20,000 British soldiers, had not made that famous march a thrust as with the point of a glittering rapier at Napoleon's flank which threatened the Emperor's communications. That audacious stroke made him stay his march through Spain a march never to be resumed while he swung round to crush the tiny but daring foe that menaced him.

Moore's strategy was, indeed, of a singularly daring quality. The Spanish armies with whom he was directed to co-operate, had simply vanished, like a cluster of eddying wind-driven leaves before a tempest. Napoleon, at the head of an apparently overwhelming force, was about to invade the rich provinces to the south, and the march of his victorious columns would not cease till their feet were wet with the waves of the Atlantic beyond Lisbon. Moore by this time had partially concentrated the scattered divisions of the British army, but his total force numbered not more than 26,000 men, of which 2000 were cavalry, with sixty guns. Moore's position was in the angle that forms the north-west shoulder, so to speak, of Spain, on Napoleon's right flank. Napoleon never doubted that Moore, when he learned the disasters which had overtaken the Spanish armies, and knew the resistless tide of war which was about to sweep across Spain to Lisbon, would instantly fall back to Corunna, or Vigo, on the sea-coast, and take ship to Lisbon. He would thus pluck his army out of deadly peril, and transport it south in readiness to meet Napoleon in front of Lisbon; if, indeed, the British Government had the courage to face the French standards there.

Moore himself, at first, resolved on that plan, but a bolder strategy took shape in his brain. He had the power of striking at Napoleon's communications with France. If he thrust boldly eastward, and menaced Napoleon's communications on the side of Burgos, he made no doubt that the Emperor would instantly swing round upon him, and a force outnumbering his by ten to one, and urged by the fiery genius of the greatest soldier of the century, would be hurled upon him. But Moore believed that he could strike at Napoleon's communications sufficiently to arrest the southward march of his columns, and so secure for Spain a breathing space, and yet pluck back his tiny army in safety before Napoleon's counter-stroke could crush it. He would draw, that is, Napoleon's whole power upon himself, would thrust his head, so as to speak, into the lion's very jaws, and yet cheat the lion's fury. As Napier puts it, he saw the peril for his own army. He knew that "it must glide along the edge of a precipice: must cross a gulf on a rotten plank; but he also knew the martial quality of his soldiers, felt the pulsation of his own genius; and, the object being worth the deed, he dared essay it even against Napoleon."

Moore was indeed a great soldier, and with better fortune might have anticipated and outshone even the fame of Wellington. He was of Scottish birth, and was one of the very finest soldiers that martial race has in modern times produced. He had a vivid, commanding personality that made him a sort of king amongst men. His eyes were dark and searching, and were set beneath a forehead of singular breadth and aspect of power. His mouth had a womanly sweetness about it, while the curve of his chin and the general contour of his face gave an extraordinary expression of energy. He lacked, perhaps, that iron quality of blood and will which augmented Wellington's capacity as a general, while it won for him an unpleasant reputation for cold-bloodedness as a friend. Moore, in fact, had a strain of gentleness in him that made him adored by his own circle. He was generous, high-minded, with a passionate scorn of base things and of base men a quality which made mean men hate him, and evil men afraid of him. Of his signal capacity for war there is no room to doubt. His ideal of soldiership was very noble, and he had the art of stamping it on all those around him.

"No man with a spark of enthusiasm," says Charles Napier, afterwards the conqueror of Scinde, "could resist the influence of Moore's great aspirings, his fine presence, his ardent penetrating genius."

Moore did more, perhaps, to create the modern British soldier than any other British general that can be named. At Shorncliffe Camp three regiments the 43rd, the 52nd, and the Rifles were under his hands. Up to that point they were commonplace regiments with no gleam of special fame about them. Moore so kindled and fashioned them that afterwards, as Wellington's famous Light Division, they were found to be "soldiers unsurpassable, perhaps never equalled." From the officers of these three regiments, who felt the breath of Moore's quickening genius, there came a longer list of notable men than has ever been yielded by any other three regiments of any service in the world. Napier says that in the list were four who afterwards commanded armies three being celebrated as conquerors above ninety who attained the rank of field officer; sixteen governors of colonies, many generals who commanded districts, &c. &c. Half-a-dozen Moores, in a word, might well have transmuted to gold the whole clay of the British army!

Napoleon himself recognised Moore's genius, when he learnt that the British commander, instead of falling back to the sea-coast, was actually striking at his communications. "Moore," he said, "is the only general now fit to contend with me; I shall advance against him in person."

Nothing could surpass the speed and energy with which Napoleon instantly changed his plans, arrested the southward march of his columns, and swung round on his daring foe. Moore on December 23 had reached Carrion, purposing to leap on Soult, who held Saldana. To beat Soult, however, was a secondary object. His real purpose was to draw Napoleon from the south, and, as Napier expresses it, "it behove the man to be alert who interposed between the lion and his prey." On December 19, 60,000 men and 150 guns were reviewed by Napoleon at the gates of Madrid, and were just being launched on that long march which was to end at Lisbon. The French light cavalry were already riding on the borders of Andalusia, the first French corps was holding Toledo. But on December 21, Napoleon heard of Moore's daring march, and within twenty-four hours his southward-moving columns were all arrested; within forty-eight hours, 50,000 French troops were at the foot of the Guadarrama Hills, the range to the northwest of Madrid, across which Napoleon must lead his troops to cut off Moore from the sea-coast.

It was winter-time. The passes were choked with snow, the cliffs were slippery with ice. Furious tempests, heavy with rain or sword-edged with sleet, howled through the ravines. Twelve hours' toil left the half frozen French columns still on the Madrid side of the mountain range, and the generals reported the passage "impossible." The leader who had crossed the St. Bernard, however, was not to be stopped by Spanish hills and snows. Napoleon, with his staff, joined the advance-guard, and, with fiery gestures and fiery speech, urged on the soldiers. Many men and many beasts perished; the struggle across the snow-filled passes lasted for two days. But Napoleon's vehemence swept all before it, and on the 24th the army had reached Villacastin, sixty miles from Madrid. On the 26th, Napoleon was at Tordesillas with the Guard, and he wrote to Soult: "Our cavalry scouts are already at Benavente. If the English pass to-day in their position, they are lost."

Napoleon, in brief, was paying back Moore with his own tactics. The British general had only to loiter on the Esla for twelve hours longer, and Napoleon would have swept like a whirlwind across his communications; and, betwixt Soult and Napoleon, the British army would have been crushed like a nut betwixt the hammer and the anvil. The speed of Napoleon's march, too, had been little less than marvellous. In the depth of winter he had executed a march of 200 miles with 50,000 men, with the energy, and something of the speed, of a thunderbolt. On December 22 he was at Madrid; on the 28th he was at Villalpando, having performed a march on bad roads, and in wild weather, of 164 miles in six days.

And yet Moore evaded him! When Napoleon reached Valdaras, the British were across the Esla; but so nicely did Moore time his movements, and with such daring did he hold on to his position in front of the converging French armies, to the very last moment, that Napoleon only missed his stroke by twelve hours, and the French cavalry scouts cut off some of the British baggage as it crossed the Esla!

Nor did Moore, indeed, begin his retreat without a brisk counter-stroke on his too eager pursuers. Thus, at Mayorga, Paget, who commanded the British cavalry, and was watching Soult, was cut off from the main body of the British by a sort of horn of cavalry thrown out from Napoleon's columns. The force falling back before Soult, that is, found solid squadrons of French horse drawn up on a hill, wet with rain, and thick with snow, on the line of its retreat. Paget led two squadrons of the 10th Hussars straight up the hill. It was stiff riding up the wet slope, and Paget halted his squadrons a few yards from the summit to give them breathing time, and then led them furiously at the enemy. With such daring did the Hussars drive their charge home that the French cavalry were smitten into fragments, and more than 100 captured. The British cavalry, it may be explained, had been for twelve days in almost hourly combat with the French outposts, and had established such a superiority over their enemies that they rode cheerfully at any odds, with an exultant certainty of success!

Napoleon urged his pursuit with amazing vehemence till he reached Astorga on January 1. His vehement will carried his troops the whole distance, from Benavente to Astorga, a distance of over thirty miles, during the brief span of a single winter's day. An icy rain beat upon the troops during the whole day, and no less than five times the infantry had to strip, and wade through the rain-swollen and snow-chilled streams. And yet they never halted. But, eagerly as Napoleon pressed on, Moore still outmarched and evaded him. At Astorga, Soult joined Napoleon, and 70,000 French infantry, 10,000 cavalry, and 200 guns were thus assembled under one command. It was an amazing proof of Napoleon's energy that, in the brief space of seven days, he should

thus have flung on Moore so mighty a force. Napoleon, to quote Napier, "had transported 50,000 men from Madrid to Astorga in less time than a Spanish courier would have taken to travel the same distance." But it was also a justification of Moore's strategy that he had thus diverted the very flower of Napoleon's forces from their march southward, to the north-west corner of Spain.

At Astorga, Napoleon was overtaken by a courier with despatches. He was galloping with the advanced posts on Moore's track, when the courier overtook him. He dismounted, ordered a bivouac fire to be lit, and cast himself down on the ground beside it to read his despatches. The snow fell heavily upon him as he read, but left him unmoved. His despatches told the Emperor that Austria had joined the league of his enemies, and that France was menaced. Napoleon's decision was swift and instant. He left Soult and Ney, with 60,000 men, to push Moore back to the sea, and, if possible, destroy him. He turned the faces of the Imperial Guard once more towards the Pyrenees, and himself rode at furious speed, and almost without escort, to Paris.

Soult, the ablest of Napoleon's marshals, pressed hard on Moore's tracks, Ney marching by a parallel route and endeavouring to turn Moore's flank. The three armies, pursuers and pursued, passed through the mountains of Galicia; but Moore, riding always with his rear-guard, kept a front of steel against his enemies, and continually evaded them.

His troops were young and inexperienced, and British soldiers, at their best, do not shine in retreat. Discipline is apt to vanish. The men grow sulky and desperate. The ordered battalions, somehow, dissolve into reckless units. And it cannot be denied that in the speed and hardship of Moore's retreat, with inexperienced officers and raw troops, the British army went sadly to pieces. The rear-guard, it is true, on which perpetual combat acted as a tonic, kept magnificently together. Discipline in it was perfect, and, as a matter of fact, it suffered less loss than the main body. For twelve days, says Napier, these hardy soldiers had covered the retreat, during which time they traversed eighty miles of road in two marches, passed several nights under arms in the snow of the mountains, and were seven times engaged. Yet they lost fewer men than any other division in the army! At Lugo, on January 7, Moore halted, and offered battle to his pursuers, and that gallant challenge, as with a touch of magic, restored discipline and cheerfulness to the British army. The stragglers, as by an electric shock, were transfigured once more into soldiers. Grumbling was silenced; battalions grew close-packed and orderly. The British soldier, at his worst, grows cheerful at the prospect of a fight, while a retreat is hateful to him. Wellington's veterans, in their famous retreat from Burgos two years afterwards, did no better than Moore's young soldiers. Soult, however, would not accept Moore's challenge of battle, and the retreat was resumed, and the pursuit urged afresh. On January 11 Corunna was reached. Moore's plan was to embark at Corunna and carry his troops to Cadiz, there to assist the Spaniards in defending the southern provinces. But when the troops reached the summit of the hills that looked down on Corunna the bay was empty! The transports were wind-bound at Vigo.

It was a marvellous retreat. Moore's marches, in all, extended over 500 miles. At one time he had no less than two great armies thundering in pursuit of him, Napoleon himself striking at his flank. Yet the English general never lost a gun, nor suffered his rear-guard to be broken; and his total losses, in spite of the temporary breakdown of the discipline of his army, were not more than 4000 men. His retreat, too, was marked with a hundred acts of daring. Again and again he turned on his pursuers, and sent their too eager squadrons staggering back with the vehemence of his counter-stroke. A charge of the 10th Hussars broke the Imperial Guard itself, slew 130, and took seventy prisoners, including their commander, General Lefebvre Desnouettes. At Villafranca, the French general, Colbert, one of Napoleon's favourite officers, was slain and his men roughly overthrown when pressing too sharply on Moore's rear. At Valladolid, Major Otway, with some British dragoons not only overthrew a French cavalry force much superior to his own, but took a colonel and more prisoners than he had men to guard.

As an example of the soldierly quality of the men who marched and fought under Moore, a single incident may be taken from Napier. At Castro Gonzalo, two privates of the 43rd, John Walton and Richard Jackson, were posted beyond the bridge, with orders that, if a force of the enemy approached, one should fire and run back to give the alarm, the other stand firm. In the grey, bitter dawn, a squadron of French cavalry, who had crept up unperceived, dashed at the two men. Jackson fired and ran, as ordered, to give the alarm. A score of horsemen in a moment were round him, slashing at him as he ran. He received fourteen sabre cuts, but, staggering, and with uniform drenched in blood, he yet ran on and gave the alarm. Walton, in turn, obeying his orders, stood at his post, a sturdy, red-coated figure, standing steadfast in a whirlwind of galloping horses and gleaming, hissing sword-strokes. Walton parried each flashing stroke as well as he could, and answered them, when possible, with a vengeful bayonet-thrust. The combat lasted for some breathless, desperate minutes; then, the British infantry coming running up, the French horsemen galloped off, leaving Walton still standing, with iron loyalty, at his post. His cap, his knapsack, his belt and musket were cut in a score of places, his bayonet was bent double, was bloody to the hilt, and notched like a saw, yet he himself was unhurt!

On January n, as we have said, Moore reached Corunna, and faced swiftly round to meet his pursuers. He was twelve hours in advance of Soult, and the French general lingered till the 16th before joining in the shock of battle a delay which was, in part, necessary to allow his straggling rearguard to close up, but in part, also, it was due to a doubt as to what might be the result of closing on a foe so hardy and stubborn. Moore employed this breathing time in preparing for embarkation. He blew up on the 13th two outlying powder magazines; in one were piled 4,000 barrels of powder, and its explosion was like the crash of a volcano. The earth trembled for miles, a tidal wave rolled across the harbour, a column of smoke and dust, with flames leaping from its back flanks, rose slowly into the sky, and then burst, pouring a roaring tempest of stones and earth over a vast area, and destroying many lives.

Moore next shot all his foundered horses, to the mingled grief and wrath of his cavalry. The 15th Hussars alone brought 400 horses into Spain, and took thirty-one back to England! The horses, it seems, were ruined, not for the want of shoes, but "for want of hammers and nails to put them on." Having embarked his dismounted cavalry, his stores, his wounded, his heavy artillery, and armed his men with new muskets, Moore quietly waited Soult's onfall. His force was only 14,000 strong, without cavalry, and with only nine six-pounders, and he could not occupy the true defence of Corunna, the great rocky range which runs at right angles to the Mero. He had to abandon this to the French, and content himself with holding an inferior ridge nearer the town.

Hope's division held the left of this ridge; Baird's the right. Paget's division was in reserve, covering the valley which curved round the western extremity of the ridge, and ran up to Corunna. Still farther to the west Fraser's division guarded the main road to Corunna. Paget's division thrust forward a battalion to the lower ranges of the hills on the western side of the valley, and then stretched a line of skirmishers across the mouth of the valley itself. Soult thus could only cross the ridge by breaking through Hope's or Baird's division. If he came up the valley he would expose his flank to Baird, and find his march barred by Paget. Moore, as a matter of fact, reckoned on his left and centre repulsing the main attack of the French; then Paget and Fraser would move up the valley and complete the French overthrow. Soult had 20,000 veteran troops and a strong artillery; and, with great skill, he planted eleven heavy guns on a rocky eminence on his left, whence they could search the whole right and centre of the British. He launched his attack in three columns the strongest, under Mermet, being intended to carry the village of Elvina, which served as an outpost to the extreme British right, and then to sweep round the right flank of Moore's position.

The onfall of the French was swift and vehement. The eleven great guns from the crags poured a tempest of shot on the British ridge, the skirmishers of Mermet's column ran forward, and drove back the British pickets with a heavy fire, while the solid column, coming on at the double after them, carried the village.

Moore, with his swift soldierly glance, instantly saw that this was the pivot of the battle, and he galloped to the spot. The 50th and the 62nd were stationed here, and Charles Napier, who as senior Major commanded the 50th, has left a most vivid word-picture of Moore's bearing on the field of battle:

I stood in front of my left wing on a knoll, from whence the greatest part of the field could be seen, and my pickets were fifty yards below, disputing the ground with the French skirmishers, but a heavy French column, which had descended the mountain at a run, was coming on behind with great rapidity, and shouting *'En avant, tue, tue, en avant, tue!'* their cannon, at the same time, plunging from above, ploughed the ground, and tore our ranks. Suddenly I heard the gallop of horses, and, turning, saw Moore. He came at speed, and pulled up so sharp and close, he seemed to have alighted from the air, man and horse looking at the approaching foe with an intentness that seemed to concentrate all feeling in their eyes. The sudden stop of the animal a cream-coloured one, with black tail and mane had cast the latter streaming forward, its ears were pushed out like horns, while it eyes flashed fire, and it snorted loudly with expanded nostrils. My first thought was, it will be away like the wind; but then I looked at the rider, and the horse was forgotten. Thrown on its haunches, the animal came sliding and dashing the dirt up with its fore-feet, thus bending the General forward almost to its neck; but his head was thrown back, and his look more keenly piercing than I ever before saw it. He glanced to the right and left, and then fixed his eyes intently on the

enemy's advancing column, at the same time grasping
the reins with both his hands, and pressing the horse
firmly with his knees; his body thus seemed to deal
with the animal while his mind was intent on the enemy, and his aspect was one of searching intenseness
beyond the power of words to describe. For a while
he looked, and then galloped to the left, without ut-
tering a word!

Moore's tactics were both daring and skilful. He swung
round the 4th Regiment, so as to smite with a flank fire
that section of the French column moving with unwise
daring round his right. He ordered up Paget, and after him
Fraser, so as to make a counter-stroke at the French left,
and meanwhile he launched the 42nd and 50th against the
French column which had carried the village in the front.
Napier, who commanded the 50th, has painted a most
graphic picture of the struggle. "Clunes," he said to the captain of the Grenadier company, "take your Grenadiers and
open the ball!"

"He stalked forward alone, like Goliath before the Philis-
tines, for six feet five he was in height, and of proportionate
bulk and strength; and thus the battle began on our side."

Napier sternly forbade any firing, and to prevent it, and
to occupy the men's attention, made them slope and carry
arms by word of command. "Many of them," he says, "cried
out 'Major, let us fire!' 'Not yet,' was my answer."

The 42nd had checked a short distance from a wall, but
Napier led his men right up to the wall, and then said:

"Do you see your enemies plainly enough to hit them?
Many voices shouted, 'By —— we do!' 'Then blaze away,'
said I; and such a rolling fire broke out as I hardly ever
heard since."

The wall was breast high. Napier, followed by the officers, leaped over, and called on the men to follow. About a hundred did so at once, and, finding the others not quick enough for his impatience, Napier leaped back, and holding a halberd horizontally pushed the men quickly over. He then leaped over himself, and the instant he did so five French soldiers suddenly rose from the ground, levelled their muskets at him, and fired! The muskets were so near as to almost touch him, but his orderly sergeant, running at his side, struck them up with his pike, and saved Napier's life.

Napier dressed his line; and, as he says, remembering the story of how the officers of the English guards at Fontenoy laid their swords over the men's firelocks to prevent them firing too high, he did the same with a halberd a curious example of how one brave act, across a hundred years, will inspire another. How Napier, with the hope of carrying the great battery, afterwards led part of his regiment up a lane lined on either side by French infantry, and so turned into a mere track of fire; how some unhappy counter-order prevented the 50th supporting him, and how Napier himself was wounded and taken prisoner cannot be told here. The story will be found, related with inimitable fire and humour, in Napier's own life.

Meanwhile, at every point, the British were victorious. The Guards and the Black Watch carried the village; Baird and Hope drove back with confusion and loss the columns that assailed them, and Moore, eagerly watching the whole line of battle from the right of his position, was about to hurl Paget, supported by Fraser, on the French left.

At that moment Moore was struck on the left breast by a cannon-ball, and dashed violently on the ground. It was a dreadful wound. The shoulder was smashed, the arm hung by a piece of skin, the ribs over the heart were stripped of flesh and broken, and the muscles that covered them hung in long rags. But Moore, absorbed in the great struggle before him, sat up in an instant, his eyes still eagerly watching Paget's advance. His staff gathered round him, and he was placed in a blanket, and some soldiers proceeded to carry him from the field. One of his staff, Hardinge, tried to unbuckle his sword, as the hilt was entangled in the strips of flesh hanging from his wound, but the dying soldier stopped him.

"I had rather," he said, "it should go out of the field with me!"

One of his officers, taking courage from Moore's unshaken countenance, expressed a hope of his recovery. Moore looked steadfastly at his own shattered breast for an instant, and calmly answered:

"No, I feel that to be impossible."

Again and again, as they carried the dying general from the field, he made his bearers halt, and turn round, that he might watch the fight. It was the scene of Wolfe on the Heights of Abraham repeated! And the spectacle was such as might well gladden the eyes of Moore. On the left, and at the centre, the British were everywhere advancing. Paget's column was overthrowing everything before it in the valley.

Had Fraser's division, as Moore intended, been brought up and frankly thrown into the fight, it can hardly be doubted that Soult would have been not merely overthrown, but destroyed. His ammunition was almost exhausted. His troops were in the mood of retreat. The Mero, a fordless river, crossed by a single bridge, was in his rear. He had lost 3,000 men; the British less than 1,000; and the British, it may be added, were full of proud and eager courage.

But Moore was dying. Baird was severely wounded. The early winter night was creeping over the field of battle, and Hope, gallant soldier though he was, judged it prudent to stay his hand. Soult had been roughly driven back; the transports were crowding into the harbour. It was enough to have ended a long retreat with the halo of victory, and to have secured an undisturbed embarkation.

Meanwhile Moore had been carried into his quarters at Corunna. A much-attached servant stood with tears running down his face as the dying man was carried into the house.

"My friend," said Moore, "it is nothing! "Then, turning to a member of his staff, Colonel Anderson, he said, "Anderson, you know I have always wished to die in this way. I hope my country will do me justice." Only once his lips quivered, and his voice shook, as he said, "Say to my mother "and then stopped, while he struggled to regain composure. "Stanhope," he said, as his eye fell on his aide-de-camp's face, "remember me to your sister" the famous Hester Stanhope, Pitt's niece, to whom Moore was engaged. Life was fast and visibly sinking, but he said, "I feel myself so strong, I fear I shall be long dying."

But he was not: death came swiftly and almost painlessly. Wrapped in a soldier's cloak he was carried by the light of torches to a grave hastily dug in the citadel at Corunna; and far off to the south, as the sorrowing officers stood round the grave of their dead chief, could be heard from time to time the sound of Soult's guns, yet in sullen retreat.

CHAPTER 2

Busaco

Busaco is, perhaps, the most picturesque of Peninsular battles. In the wild nature of the ground over which it raged, the dramatic incidents which marked its progress, the furious daring of the assault, and the stern valour of the defence, it is almost without a rival. The French had every advantage in the fight, save one. They were 65,000 strong, an army of veterans, many of them the men of Austerlitz and Marengo. Massena led; Ney was second in command; both facts being pledges of daring generalship. The English were falling sullenly back in the long retreat which ended at Torres Vedras, and the French were in exultant pursuit. Massena had announced that he was going to "drive the leopard into the sea"; and French soldiers, it may be added, are never so dangerous as when on fire with the *élan* of success.

Wellington's army was inferior to its foe in numbers, and of mixed nationality, and it is probable that retreat had loosened the fibre of even British discipline, if not of British courage. Two days before Busaco, for example, the light division, the very flower of the English army, was encamped in a pine-wood about which a peasant had warned them that it was "haunted." During the night, without signal or visible cause, officers and men, as though suddenly smitten with frenzy, started from their sleep and dispersed in all directions. Nor could the mysterious panic be stayed until some officer, shrewder than the rest, shouted the order, "Prepare to receive cavalry," when the instinct of discipline asserted itself, the men rushed into rallying squares, and, with huge shouts of laughter, recovered themselves from their panic.

But battle is to the British soldier a tonic, and when Wellington drew up his lines in challenge of battle to his pursuer, on the great hill of Busaco, his red-coated soldiery were at least full of a grim satisfaction. One of the combatants has described the diverse aspects of the two hosts on the night before the fight. "The French were all bustle and gaiety; but along the whole English line the soldiers, in stern silence, examined their flints, cleaned their locks and barrels, and then stretched themselves on the ground to rest, each with his firelock within his grasp." The single advantage of the British lay in their position. Busaco is a great hill, one of the loftiest and most rugged in Portugal, eight miles in breadth, and barring the road by which Massena was moving on Lisbon. "There are certainly," said Wellington, "many bad roads in Portugal, but the enemy has taken decidedly the worst in the whole kingdom."

The great ridge, with its gloomy tree-clad heights and cloven crest, round which the mists hung in sullen vapour, was an ideal position for defence. In its front was a valley forming a natural ditch so deep that the eye could scarcely pierce its depths. The ravine at one point was so narrow that the English and French guns waged duel across it, but on the British side the chasm was almost perpendicular.

From their eyrie perch on September 27, 1810, the English watched Massena's great host coming on. Every emi-

nence sparkled with their bayonets, every road was crowded with their wagons; it seemed not so much the march of
an army as the movement of a nation. The vision of "grim
Busaco's iron ridge," glittering with bayonets, arrested the
march of the French. But Ney, whose military glance was
keen and sure, saw that the English arrangements were not
yet complete; an unfilled gap, three miles wide, parted the
right wing from the left, and he was eager for an immediate attack. Massena, however, was ten miles in the rear.
According to Marbot, who has left a spirited account of
Busaco, Massena put off the attack till the next day, and
thus threw away a great opportunity. In the gloomy depths
of the ravines, however, a war of skirmishers broke out,
and the muskets rang loudly through the echoing valleys,
while the puffs of eddying white smoke rose through the
black pines. But night fell, and the mountain heights above
were crowned with the bivouac fires of 100,000 warriors,
over whom the serene sky glittered. Presently a bitter wind
broke on the mountain summits, and all through the night
the soldiers shivered under its keen blast.

Massena's plan of attack was simple and daring. Ney was
to climb the steep front on the English left, and assail the
light division under Craufurd; Regnier, with a *corps d'élite*,
was to attack the English left, held by Picton's division.
Regnier formed his attack into five columns while the stars
were yet glittering coldly in the morning sky. They had first
to plunge into the savage depths of the ravine, and then
climb the steep slope leading to the English position. The
vigour of the attack was magnificent. General Merle, who
had won fame at Austerlitz, personally led the charge. At a
run the columns went down the ravine; at a run, scarcely
less swift, they swept up the hostile slope. The guns smote

the columns from end to end, and the attack left behind it a broad crimson trail of the dead and dying. But it never paused. A wave of steel and fire and martial tumult, it swept up the hill, broke over the crest in a spray of flame, brushed aside a Portuguese regiment in its path like a wisp of straw, and broke on the lines of the third division.

The pressure was too great for even the solid English line to sustain; it, too, yielded to the impetuous French, part of whom seized the rocks at the highest point of the hill, while another part wheeled to the right, intending to sweep the summit of the sierra. It was an astonishing feat. Only French soldiers, magnificently led and in a mood of victory, could have done it; and only British soldiers, it may be added, whom defeat hardens, could have restored such a reverse.

Picton was in command, and he sent at the French a wing of the 88th, the famous Connaught Rangers, led by Colonel Wallace, an officer in whom Wellington reposed great confidence. Wallace's address was brief and pertinent. "Press them to the muzzle, Connaught Rangers; press on to the rascals." There is no better fighting material in the world than an Irish regiment well led and in a high state of discipline, and this matchless regiment, with levelled bayonets, ran in on the French with a grim and silent fury there was no denying. Vain was resistance. Marbot says of the Rangers that "their first volley, delivered at fifteen paces, stretched more than 500 men on the ground"; and the threatening gleam of the bayonet followed fiercely on the flame of the musket.

The French were borne, shouting, struggling, and fighting desperately, over the crest and down the deep slope to the ravine below. In a whirlwind of dust and fire and

clamour went the whole body of furious soldiery into the valley, leaving a broad track of broken arms and dying men. According to the regimental records of the 88th, "Twenty minutes sufficed to teach the heroes of Marengo and Austerlitz that they must yield to the Rangers of Connaught!" As the breathless Rangers re-formed triumphantly on the ridge, Wellington galloped up and declared he had never witnessed a more gallant charge.

But a wing of Regnier's attack had formed at right angles across the ridge. It was pressing forward with stern resolution; it swept before it the light companies of the 74th and 88th regiments, and unless this attack could be arrested the position and the battle were lost. Picton rallied his broken lines within *sixty yards* of the French muskets, a feat not the least marvellous in a marvellous fight, and then sent them furiously at the exulting French, who held a strong position amongst the rocks. It is always difficult to disentangle the confusion which marks a great fight. Napier says that it was Cameron who formed line with the 38th under a violent fire, and, without returning a shot, ran in upon the French grenadiers with the bayonet and hurled them triumphantly over the crest. Picton, on the other hand, declares that it was the light companies of the 74th and the 88th, under Major Smith, an officer of great daring—who fell in the moment of victory—that flung the last French down over the cliff. Who can decide when such experts, and actors in the actual scene, differ?

The result, however, as seen from the French side, is clear. The French, Marbot records, "found themselves driven in a heap down the deep descent up which they had climbed, and the English lines followed them halfway down firing murderous volleys. At this point we lost a general, 2 colonels, 80 officers, and 700 or 800 men." "The English," he adds in explanation of this dreadful loss of life, "were the best marksmen in Europe, the only troops who were perfectly practised in the use of small arms, whence their firing was far more accurate than that of any other infantry."

A gleam of humour at this point crosses the grim visage of battle. Picton, on lying down in his bivouac the night before the battle, had adorned his head with a picturesque and highly coloured nightcap. The sudden attack of the French woke him; he clapped on cloak and cocked hat, and rode to the fighting line, when he personally led the attack which flung the last of Regnier's troops down the slope. At the moment of the charge he took off his cocked hat to wave the troops onward; this revealed the domestic head-dress he unconsciously wore, and the astonished soldiers beheld their general on flame with warlike fury gesticulating martially in a nightcap! A great shout of laughter went up from the men as they stopped for a moment to realise the spectacle; then with a tempest of mingled laughter and cheers they flung themselves on the enemy.

Meanwhile Ney had formed his attack on the English left, held by Craufurd and the famous light division. Marbot praises the characteristic tactics of the British in such fights. "After having, as we do," he says, "garnished their front with skirmishers, they post their principal forces out of sight, holding them all the time sufficiently near to the key of the position to be able to attack the enemy the instant they reach it; and this attack, made unexpectedly on assailants who have lost heavily, and think the victory already theirs, succeeds almost invariably." "We had," he adds, "a melancholy experience of this art at Busaco." Craufurd, a soldier of fine skill, made exactly such a disposition of his men. Some rocks at the edge of the ravine formed natural embrasures for the English guns under Ross; below them the Rifles were flung out as skirmishers; behind them the German infantry were the only visible troops; but in a fold of the hill, unseen, Craufurd held the 43rd and 52nd regiments drawn up in line.

Ney's attack, as might be expected, was sudden and furious. The English, in the grey dawn, looking down the ravine, saw three huge masses start from the French lines and swarm up the slope. To climb an ascent so steep, vexed by skirmishers on either flank, and scourged by the guns which flashed from the summit, was a great and most daring feat—yet the French did it. Busaco, indeed, is memorable as showing the French fighting quality at its highest point. General Simon led Loison's attack right up to the lips of the English guns, and in the dreadful charge its order was never disturbed nor its speed arrested. "Ross's guns," says Napier, "were worked with incredible quickness, yet their range was palpably contracted every round; the enemy's shot came singing up in a sharper key; the English skirmishers, breathless and begrimed with powder, rushed over the edge of the ascent; the artillery drew back"—and over the edge of the hill came the bearskins and the gleaming bayonets of the French! General Simon led the attack so fiercely home that he was the first to leap across the English entrenchments, when an infantry soldier, lingering stubbornly after his comrades had fallen back, shot him point-blank through the face. The unfortunate general, when the fight was over, was found lying in the redoubt amongst the dying and the dead, with scarcely a human feature left. He recovered, was sent as a prisoner to England, and was afterwards exchanged, but his horrible wound made it impossible for him to serve again.

Craufurd had been watching meanwhile with grim coolness the onward rush of the French. They came storming and exultant, a wave of martial figures, edged with a spray of fire and a tossing fringe of bayonets, over the summit of the hill; when suddenly Craufurd, in a shrill tone, called on his reserves to attack. In an instant there rose, as if out of the ground, before the eyes of the astonished French, the serried lines of the 43rd and 52nd, and what a moment before was empty space was now filled with the frowning visage of battle. The British lines broke into one stern and deep-toned shout, and 1800 bayonets, in one long line of gleaming points, came swiftly down upon the French. To stand against that moving hedge of deadly and level steel was impossible; yet each man in the leading section of the French raised his musket and fired, and two officers and ten soldiers fell before them. Not a Frenchman had missed his mark! They could do no more. "The head of their column," to quote Napier, "was violently thrown back upon the rear, both flanks were overlapped at the same moment by the English wings, and three terrible discharges at five yards' distance shattered the wavering mass." Before those darting points of flame the pride of the French shrivelled. Shining victory was converted, in almost the passage of an instant, into bloody defeat; and a shattered mass, with ranks broken, and colours abandoned, and discipline forgotten, the French were swept into the depths of the ravine out of which they had climbed.

One of the dramatic episodes of the fight at this juncture is that of Captain Jones—known in his regiment as "Jack

Jones" of the 52nd. Jones was a fiery Welshman, and led his company in the rush on General Simon's column. The French were desperately trying to deploy, a *chef-de-bataillon* giving the necessary orders with great vehemence. Jones ran ahead of his charging men, outstripping them by speed of foot, challenged the French officer with a warlike gesture to single combat, and slew him with one fierce thrust before his own troops, and the 52nd, as they came on at the run, saw the duel and its result, were lifted by it to a mood of victory, and raised a sudden shout of exultation, which broke the French as by a blast of musketry fire.

For hours the battle spluttered and smouldered amongst the skirmishers in the ravines, and some gallant episodes followed. Towards evening, for example, a French company, with signal audacity, and apparently on its own private impulse, seized a cluster of houses only half a musket shot from the light division, and held it while Craufurd scourged them with the fire of twelve guns. They were only turned out at the point of the bayonet by the 43rd. But the battle was practically over, and the English had beaten, by sheer hard fighting, the best troops and the best marshals of France.

In the fierceness of actual fighting, Busaco has never been surpassed, and seldom did the wounded and dying lie thicker on a battlefield than where the hostile lines struggled together on that fatal September 27. The *melée* at some points was too close for even the bayonet to be used, and the men fought with fists or with the butt-end of their muskets. From the rush which swept Regnier's men down the slope the Connaught Rangers came back with faces and hands and weapons literally splashed red with blood. The firing was so fierce that Wellington, with his whole staff, dismounted. Napier, however—one of the famous fighting trio of that name, who afterwards conquered Scinde—fiercely refused to dismount, or even cover his red uniform with a cloak. "This is the uniform of my regiment," he said, "and in it I will show, or fall this day." He had scarcely uttered the words when a bullet smashed through his face and shattered his jaw to pieces. As he was carried past Lord Wellington he waved his hand and whispered through his torn mouth, "I could not die at a better moment!" Of such stuff were the men who fought under Wellington in the Peninsula.

CHAPTER 3

Albuera

Albuera is the fiercest, bloodiest, and most amazing fight in the mighty drama of the Peninsular war. On May 11, 1811, the English guns were thundering sullenly over Badajos. Wellington was beyond the Guadiana, pressing Marmont; and Beresford, with much pluck but little skill, was besieging the great frontier fortress. Soult, however, a master of war, was swooping down from Seville to raise the siege. On the 14th he reached Villafranca, only thirty miles distant, and fired salvos from his heaviest guns all through the night to warn the garrison of approaching succour. Beresford could not both maintain the siege and fight Soult; and on the night of the 13th he abandoned his trenches, burnt his gabions and fascines, and marched to meet Soult at Albuera, a low ridge, with a shallow river in front, which barred the road to Badajos. As the morning of May 16, 1811, broke, heavy with clouds, and wild with gusty rainstorms, the two armies grimly gazed at each other in stern pause, ere they joined in the wrestle of actual battle.

All the advantages, save one, were on the side of the French. Soult was the ablest of the French marshals. If he had not Ney's *élan* in attack, or Massena's stubborn resource in retreat, yet he had a military genius, since Lannes was dead, second only to that of Napoleon himself. He had under his command 20,000 war-hardened infantry, 40 guns, and 4000 magnificent cavalry, commanded by Latour Maubourg, one of the most brilliant of French cavalry generals. Beresford, the British commander, had the dogged fighting courage, half Dutch and half English, of his name and blood; but as a commander he was scarcely third-rate. Of his army of 30,000, 15,000 were Spanish, half drilled, and more than half starved—they had lived for days on horse-flesh—under Blake, a general who had lost all the good qualities of Irish character, and acquired all the bad ones peculiar to Spanish temper. Of Beresford's remaining troop 8000 were Portuguese; he had only 7000 British soldiers.

Beresford ought not to have fought. He had abandoned the siege at Badajos, and no reason for giving battle remained. The condition of Blake's men, no doubt, made retreat difficult. They had reached the point at which they must either halt or lie down and die. The real force driving Beresford to battle, however, was the fighting effervescence in his own blood and the warlike impatience of his English troops. They had taken no part in the late great battles under Wellington; Busaco had been fought and Fuentes de Onoro gained without them; and they were in the mood, both officers and men, of fierce determination to fight *somebody*! This was intimated somewhat roughly to Beresford, and he had not that iron ascendency over his troops Wellington possessed. As a matter of fact, he was himself as stubbornly eager to fight as any private in the ranks.

The superiority of Soult's warlike genius was shown before a shot was fired. Beresford regarded the bridge that crossed the Albuera and the village that clustered at the

bridge-head as the key of his position. He occupied the village with Alten's German brigade, covered the bridge with the fire of powerful batteries, and held in reserve above it his best British brigade, the fusiliers, under Cole, the very regiments who, four hours later, on the extreme right of Beresford's position, were actually to win the battle. Soult's sure vision, however, as he surveyed his enemies on the evening of the 15th, saw that Beresford's right was his weak point. It was a rough, broken table-land, curving till it looked into the rear of Beresford's line. It was weakly held by Blake and his Spaniards. Immediately in its front was a low wooded hill, behind which, as a screen, an attacking force could be gathered.

In the night Soult placed behind this hill the fifth corps, under Gerard, the whole of his cavalry, under Latour Maubourg, and the strength of his artillery. When the morning broke, Soult had 15,000 men and 30 guns within ten minutes' march of Beresford's right wing, and nobody suspected it. No gleam of colour, no murmur of packed battalions, no ring of steel, no sound of marching feet warned the deluded English general of the battle-storm about to break on his right wing. A commander with such an unexpected tempest ready to burst on the weakest point of his line was by all the rules of war pre-doomed.

At nine o'clock Soult launched an attack at the bridge, the point where Beresford expected him, but it was only a feint. Beresford, however, with all his faults, had the soldierly brain to which the actual thunder of the cannon gave clearness. He noticed that the French battalions supporting the attack on the bridge did not press on closely. As a matter of fact, as soon as the smoke of artillery from the battle raging at the bridge swept over the field, they swung smartly to the left, and at the double hastened to add themselves to the thunderbolt which Soult was launching at Beresford's right. But Beresford, meanwhile, had guessed Soult's secret, and he sent officer after officer ordering and entreating Blake to change front so as to meet Soult's attack on his flank, and he finally rode thither himself to enforce his commands. Blake, however, was immovable through pride, and his men through sheer physical weakness. They could die, but they could not march or deploy. Blake at last tried to change front, but as he did so the French attack smote him. Pressing up the gentle rise, Gerard's men scourged poor Blake's flank with their fire; the French artillery, coming swiftly on, halted every fifty yards to thunder on the unhappy Spaniards; while Latour Maubourg's lancers and hussars, galloping in a wider sweep, gathered momentum for a wild ride on Blake's actual rear.

Beresford tried to persuade the Spaniards to charge as the French were thus circling round them. Shouts and gesticulations were in vain. He was a man of giant height and strength, and he actually seized a Spanish ensign in his iron grip, and carried him bodily, flag and all, at a run for fifty yards towards the moving French lines, and planted him there. When released, however, the bewildered Spaniard simply took to his heels and ran back to his friends, as a terrified sheep might run back to the flock. In half-an-hour Beresford's battle had grown desperate. Two-thirds of the French, in compact order of battle, were perpendicular to his right; the Spaniards were falling into disorder. Soult saw the victory in his grasp, and eagerly pushed forward his reserves. Over the whole hill, mingled with furious blasts of rain, rolled the tumult of a disorderly and broken fight. Ten minutes more would have enabled Soult to fling Beresford's

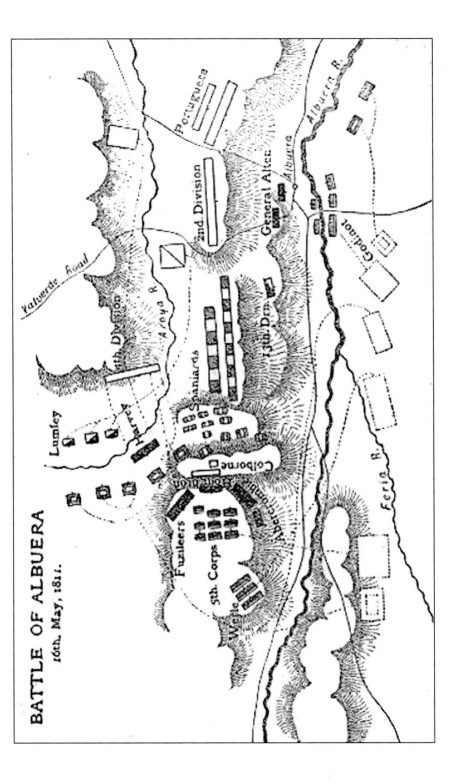

BATTLE OF ALBUERA
16th. May, 1811.

right, a shattered and routed mass, on the only possible line of retreat, and with the French superiority in cavalry his army would have been blotted out.

The share of the British in the fight consisted of three great attacks delivered by way of counter-stroke to Soult's overwhelming rush on the hill held by Blake. The first attack was delivered by the second division, under Colborne, led by General Stewart in person. Stewart was a sort of British version of Ney, a man of vehement spirit, with a daring that grew even more flame-like in the eddying tumult and tempest of actual battle. He saw Soult's attack crumpling up Blake's helpless battalions, while the flash of the French artillery every moment grew closer. It was the crisis of the fight, and Stewart brought on Colborne's men at a run. Colborne himself, a fine soldier with cool judgment, wished to halt and form his men in order of battle before plunging into the confused vortex of the fight above; but Stewart, full of breathless ardour, hurried the brigade up the hill in column of companies, reached the Spanish right, and began to form line by succession of battalions as they arrived.

At this moment a wild tempest of rain was sweeping over the British as, at the double, they came up the hill; the eddying fog, thick and slab with the smoke of powder, hid everything twenty yards from the panting soldiers. Suddenly the wall of changing fog to their right sparkled into swiftly moving spots of red; it shone the next instant with the gleam of a thousand steel points; above the thunder of the cannon, the shouts of contending men, rose the awful sound of a tempest of galloping hoofs. The French lancers and hussars caught the English in open order, and in five fierce and bloody minutes almost trampled them out

of· existence! Two-thirds of the brigade went down. The
31st Regiment flung itself promptly into square, and stood
fast—a tiny island, edged with steel and flame, amid the
mad tumult; but the French lancers, drunk with excite-
ment, mad with battle fury, swept over the whole slope of
the hill. They captured six guns, and might have done yet
more fatal mischief but that they occupied themselves in
galloping to and fro across the line of their original charge,
spearing the wounded.

One lancer charged Beresford as he sat, solitary and huge,
on his horse amid the broken English regiments. But Beresford was at least a magnificent trooper; he put the lance aside
with one hand, and caught the Frenchman by the throat,
lifted him clean from his saddle, and dashed him senseless
on the ground! The ensign who carried the colours of the
3rd Buffs covered them with his body till he was slain by a
dozen lance-thrusts; the ensign who carried the other colours of the same regiment tore the flag from its staff and
thrust it into his breast, and it was found there, stiff with his
blood, after the fight. The Spaniards, meanwhile, were firing
incessantly but on general principles merely, and into space
or into the ranks of their own allies as might happen; and
the 29th, advancing to the help of Colborne's broken men,
finding the Spaniards in their path and firing into their lines,
broke sternly into volleys on them in turn. Seldom has a
battlefield witnessed a tumult so distracted and wild.

The first English counter-stroke had failed, but the second followed swiftly. The furious rain and fog which had
proved so fatal to Colborne's men for a moment, was in
favour of Beresford. Soult, though eagerly watching the
conflict, could not see the ruin into which the British had
fallen, and hesitated to launch his reserves into the fight.

The 31st still sternly held its own against the French cavalry, and this gave time for Stewart to bring up Houghton's brigade. But this time Stewart, though he brought up his men with as much vehemence as before, brought them up in order of battle. The 29th, the 48th, and the 57th swept up the hill in line, led by Houghton, hat in hand. He fell, pierced by three bullets; but over his dead body, eager to close, the British line still swept. They reached the crest. A deep and narrow ravine arrested their bayonet charge; but with stubborn valour they held the ground they had gained, scourged with musketry fire at pistol-shot distance, and by artillery at fifty yards' range, while a French column smote them with its musketry on their flank. The men fell fast, but fought as they fell. Stewart was twice wounded; Colonel Dutworth, of the 48th, slain; of the 57th, out of 570 men, 430, with their colonel, Inglis, fell. The men, after the battle, were found lying dead in ranks exactly as they fought. "Die hard! my men, die hard!" said Inglis when the bullet struck him; and the 57th have borne the name of "Die hards" ever since. At Inkerman, indeed, more than fifty years afterwards, the "Die hard!" of Inglis served to harden the valour of the 57th in a fight as stern as Albuera itself.

But ammunition began to fail. Houghton's men would not yield, but it was plain that in a few more minutes there would be none of them left, save the dead and the wounded. And at this dreadful moment Beresford, distracted with the tumult and horror of the fight, wavered! He called up Alten's men from the bridge to cover his retreat, and prepared to yield the fatal hill. At this juncture, however, a mind more masterful and daring than his own launched a third British attack against the victorious French and won the dreadful day.

Colonel Hardinge, afterwards famous in Indian battles, acted as quartermaster-general of the Portuguese army; on his own responsibility he organised the third English attack. Cole had just come up the road from Badajos with two brigades, and Hardinge urged him to lead his men straight up the hill; then riding to Abercrombie's brigade, he ordered him to sweep round the flank of the hill. Beresford, on learning of this movement, accepted it, and sent back Alten's men to retake the bridge which they had abandoned.

Abercrombie's men swept to the left of the hill, and Cole, a gallant and able soldier, using the Portuguese regiments in his brigade as a guard against a flank attack of the French cavalry, led his two fusilier regiments, the 7th and 23rd, straight to the crest.

At this moment the French reserves were coming on, the fragments of Houghton's brigade were falling back, the field was heaped with carcases, the lancers were riding furiously about the captured artillery, and with a storm of exultant shouts the French were sweeping on to assured victory. It was the dramatic moment of the fight. Suddenly through the fog, coming rapidly on with stern faces and flashing volleys, appeared the long line of Cole's fusiliers on the right of Houghton's staggering groups, while at the same exact moment Abercrombie's line broke through the mist on their left. As these grim and threatening lines became visible, the French shouts suddenly died down. It was the old contest of the British line—the "thin red line"—against the favourite French attack in column, and the story can only be told in Napier's resonant prose. The passage which describes the attack of the fusiliers is one of the classic passages of English battle literature, and in its syllables can still almost be heard the tread of marching feet, the shrill clangour of smitten steel, and the thunder of the musketry volleys:

Such a gallant line, arising from amid the smoke, and rapidly separating itself from the confused and broken multitude, startled the enemy's masses, which were increasing and pressing forward as to assured victory; they wavered, hesitated, and then, vomiting forth a storm of fire, hastily endeavoured to enlarge their front, while the fearful discharge of grape from all their artillery whistled through the British ranks. Myers was killed. Cole and the three colonels—Ellis, Blakeney, and Hawkshawe—fell wounded, and the fusilier battalions, struck by the iron tempest, reeled and staggered like sinking ships. Suddenly and sternly recovering, they closed on their terrible enemies, and then was seen with what a strength and majesty the British soldier fights. In vain did Soult, by voice and gesture, animate his Frenchmen; in vain did the hardiest veterans break from the crowded columns and sacrifice their lives to gain time for the mass to open on such a fair field; in vain did the mass itself bear up, and, fiercely striving, fire indiscriminately on friends and foes, while the horsemen, hovering on the flanks, threatened to charge the advancing line.

Nothing could stop that astonishing infantry. No sudden burst of undisciplined valour, no nervous enthusiasm weakened the stability of their order; their flashing eyes were bent on the dark columns in front, their measured tread shook the ground, their dreadful volleys swept away the head of every formation, their deafening shouts overpowered the dissonant cries that broke from all parts of the tumultuous crowd as slowly and with a horrid carnage it was driven by the incessant vigour of the attack to the farthest edge of the hill. In vain did the French reserves mix with the struggling multitude to sustain the fight; their efforts only increased the irremediable confusion, and the mighty mass, breaking off like a loosened cliff, went headlong down the ascent. The rain flowed after in streams discoloured with blood, and 1800 unwounded men, the remnant of 6000 unconquerable British soldiers, stood triumphant on the fatal hill.

The battle of Albuera lasted four hours; its slaughter was dreadful. Within the space of a few hundred feet square were strewn some 7000 bodies, and over this Aceldama the artillery had galloped, the cavalry had charged! The 3rd Buffs went into the fight with 24 officers and 750 rank and file; at the roll-call next morning there were only 5 officers and 35 men. One company of the Royal Fusiliers came out of the fight commanded by a corporal; every officer and sergeant had been killed. Albuera is essentially a soldier's fight. The bayonet of the private, not the brain of the general, won it; and never was the fighting quality of our race more brilliantly shown. Soult summed up the battle in words that deserve to be memorable. "There is no beating those troops," he wrote, "*in spite of their generals!*"

"I always thought them bad soldiers," he added, with a Frenchman's love of paradox; "now I am sure of it. For I turned their right, pierced their centre, they were everywhere broken, the day was mine, and yet *they did not know it*, and would not run!"

CHAPTER 4
Ciudad Rodrigo

The three great and memorable sieges of the Peninsular war are those of Ciudad Rodrigo, Badajos, and San Sebastian. The annals of battle record nowhere a more furious daring in assault or a more gallant courage in defence than that which raged in turn round each of these three great fortresses. Of the three sieges that of Badajos was the most picturesque and bloody; that of San Sebastian the most sullen and exasperated; that of Ciudad Rodrigo the swiftest and most brilliant. A great siege tests the fighting quality of any army as nothing else can test it. In the night watches in the trenches, in the dogged toil of the batteries, and the crowded perils of the breach, all the frippery and much of the real discipline of an army dissolves. The soldiers fall back upon what may be called the primitive fighting qualities—the hardihood of the individual soldier, the daring with which the officers will lead, the dogged loyalty with which the men will follow. As an illustration of the warlike qualities in our race by which empire has been achieved, nothing better can be desired than the story of how the breaches were won at Ciudad Rodrigo.

At the end of 1811 the English and the French were watching each other jealously across the Spanish border. The armies of Marmont and of Soult, 67,000 strong, lay within touch of each other, barring Wellington's entrance into Spain. Wellington, with 35,000 men, of whom not more than 10,000 men were British, lay within sight of the Spanish frontier. It was the winter time. Wellington's army was wasted by sickness, his horses were dying of mere starvation, his men had received no pay for three months, and his muleteers none for eight months. He had no siege-train, his regiments were ragged and hungry, and the French generals confidently reckoned the British army as, for the moment at least, *une quantité négligeable*.

And yet at that precise moment, Wellington, subtle and daring, was meditating a leap upon the great frontier fortress of Ciudad Rodrigo, in the Spanish province of Salamanca. Its capture would give him a safe base of operations against Spain; it was the great frontier *place d'armes* for the French; the whole siege-equipage, and stores of the army of Portugal were contained in it. The problem of how, in the depth of winter, without materials for a siege, to snatch a place so strong from under the very eyes of two armies, each stronger than his own, was a problem which might have taxed the warlike genius of a Caesar. But Wellington accomplished it with a combination of subtlety and audacity simply marvellous.

He kept the secret of his design so perfectly that his own engineers never suspected it, and his adjutant-general, Murray, went home on leave without dreaming anything was going to happen. Wellington collected artillery ostensibly for the purpose of arming Almeida, but the guns were trans-shipped at sea and brought secretly to the mouth of the Douro. No less than 800 mule-carts were constructed without anybody guessing their purpose. Wellington, while these preparations were on foot, was keenly watching Marmont and Soult, till he saw that they were lulled into a state of mere yawning security, and then, in Napier's expressive phrase, he "instantly jumped with both feet upon Ciudad Rodrigo."

This famous fortress, in shape, roughly resembles a triangle with the angles truncated. The base, looking to the south, is covered by the Agueda, a river given to sudden inundations; the fortifications were strong and formidably armed; as outworks it had to the east the great fortified Convent of San Francisco, to the west a similar building called Santa Cruz; whilst almost parallel with the northern face rose two rocky ridges called the Great and Small Teson, the nearest within 600 yards of the city ramparts, and crowned by a formidable redoubt called Francisco. The siege began on January 8. The soil was rocky and covered with snow, the nights were black, the weather bitter. The men lacked entrenching tools. They had to encamp on the side of the Agueda farthest from the city, and ford that river every time the trenches were relieved. The 1st, 3rd, and light divisions formed the attacking force; each division held the trenches in turn for twenty-four hours. Let the reader imagine what degree of hardihood it took to wade in the grey and bitter winter dawn through a half-frozen river, and without fire or warm food, and under a ceaseless rain of shells from the enemy's guns, to toil in the frozen trenches, or to keep watch, while the icicles hung from eyebrow and beard, over the edge of the battery for twenty-four hours in succession.

Nothing in this great siege is more wonderful than the fierce speed with which Wellington urged his operations. Massena, who had besieged and captured the city the year before in the height of summer, spent a month in bombarding it before he ventured to assault. Wellington broke ground on January 8th, under a tempest of mingled hail and rain; he stormed it on the night of the 19th.

He began operations by leaping on the strong work that crowned the Great Teson the very night the siege began. Two companies from each regiment of the light division were detailed by the officer of the day, Colonel Colborne, for the assault. Colborne (afterwards Lord Seaton), a cool and gallant soldier, called his officers together in a group and explained with great minuteness how they were to attack. He then launched his men against the redoubt with a vehemence so swift that, to those who watched the scene under the light of a wintry moon, the column of redcoats, like the thrust of a crimson sword-blade, spanned the ditch, shot up the glacis, and broke through the parapet with a single movement. The accidental explosion of a French shell burst the gate open, and the remainder of the attacking party instantly swept through it. There was fierce musketry fire and a tumult of shouting for a moment or two, but in twenty minutes from Colborne's launching his attack every Frenchman in the redoubt was killed, wounded, or a prisoner.

The fashion in which the gate was blown open was very curious. A French sergeant was in the act of throwing a live shell upon the storming party in the ditch, when he was struck by an English bullet. The lighted shell fell from his hands within the parapet, was kicked away by the nearest French in mere self-preservation; it rolled towards the gate, exploded, burst it open, and instantly the British broke in.

For ten days a desperate artillery duel raged between the besiegers and the besieged. The parallels were resolutely pushed on in spite of rocky soil, broken tools, bitter

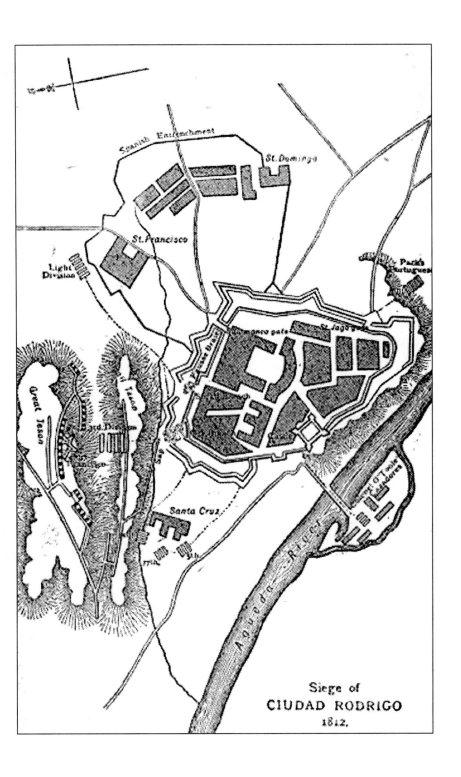

Siege of
CIUDAD RODRIGO
1812.

weather, and the incessant pelting of the French guns. The temper of the British troops is illustrated by an incident which George Napier—the youngest of the three Napiers—relates. The three others were gallant and remarkable soldiers. Charles Napier in India and elsewhere made history; William, in his wonderful tale of the Peninsular war, wrote history; and George, if he had not the literary genius of the one nor the strategic skill of the other, was a most gallant soldier.

I was a field-officer of the trenches," he says, "when a 13-inch shell from the town fell in the midst of us. I called to the men to lie down flat, and they instantly obeyed orders, except one of them, an Irishman and an old marine, but a most worthless drunken dog, who trotted up to the shell, the fuse of which was still burning, and striking it with his spade, knocked the fuse out; then taking the immense shell in his hands, brought it to me, saying, 'There she is for you now, yer 'anner. I've knocked the life out of the crater.'

The besieged brought fifty heavy guns to reply to the thirty light pieces by which they were assailed, and day and night the bellow of eighty pieces boomed sullenly over the doomed city and echoed faintly back from the nearer hills, while the walls crashed to the stroke of the bullet. The English fire made up by fierceness and accuracy for what it lacked in weight; but the sap made no progress, the guns showed signs of being worn out, and although two apparent breaches had been made, the counterscarp was not destroyed. Yet Wellington determined to attack, and, in his characteristic fashion, to attack by night. The siege had lasted ten days, and Marmont, with an army stronger than his own, was lying within four marches. That he had not appeared already on the scene was wonderful.

In a general order issued on the evening of the 19th Wellington wrote, "Ciudad Rodrigo must be stormed this evening." The great breach was a sloping gap in the wall at its northern angle, about a hundred feet wide. The French had crowned it with two guns loaded with grape; the slope was strewn with bombs, hand-grenades, and bags of powder; a great mine pierced it beneath; a deep ditch had been cut betwixt the breach and the adjoining ramparts, and these were crowded with riflemen. The third division, under General Mackinnon, was to attack the breach, its forlorn hope being led by Ensign Mackie, its storming party by General Mackinnon himself. The lesser breach was a tiny gap, scarcely twenty feet wide, to the left of the great breach; this was to be attacked by the light division, under Craufurd, its forlorn hope of twenty-five men being led by Gurwood, and its storming party by George Napier. General Pack, with a Portuguese brigade, was to make a sham attack on the eastern face, while a fourth attack was to be made on the southern front by a company of the 83rd and some Portuguese troops. In the storming party of the 83rd were the Earl of March, afterwards Duke of Richmond; Lord Fitzroy Somerset, afterwards Lord Raglan; and the Prince of Orange—all volunteers without Wellington's knowledge!

At 7 o'clock a curious silence fell suddenly on the battered city and the engirdling trenches. Not a light gleamed from the frowning parapets, not a murmur arose from the blackened trenches. Suddenly a shout broke out on the right of the English attack; it ran, a wave of stormy sound, along the line of the trenches. The men who were to at-

tack the great breach leaped into the open. In a moment
the space betwixt the hostile lines was covered with the
stormers, and the gloomy half-seen face of the great fortress
broke into a tempest of fire.

Nothing could be finer than the vehement courage of
the assault, unless it were the cool and steady fortitude of
the defence. Swift as was the upward rush of the stormers,
the race of the 5th, 77th, and 94th regiments was almost
swifter. Scorning to wait for the ladders, they leaped into
the great ditch, outpaced even the forlorn hope, and pushed
vehemently up the great breach, whilst their red ranks were
torn by shell and shot. The fire, too, ran through the tangle
of broken stones over which they climbed; the hand-grenades and powder-bags by which it was strewn exploded.
The men were walking on fire! Yet the attack could not
be denied. The Frenchmen—shooting, stabbing, yelling—
were driven behind their entrenchments. There the fire of
the houses commanding the breach came to their help, and
they made a gallant stand. "None would go back on either
side, and yet the British could not get forward, and men
and officers falling in heaps choked up the passage, which
from minute to minute was raked with grape from two
guns flanking the top of the breach at the distance of a few
yards. Thus striving, and trampling alike upon the dead and
the wounded, these brave men maintained the combat."

It was the attack on the smaller breach which really
carried Ciudad Rodrigo; and George Napier, who led it,
has left a graphic narrative of the exciting experiences of
that dreadful night. The light division was to attack, and
Craufurd, with whom Napier was a favourite, gave him
command of the storming party. He was to ask for 100
volunteers from each of the three British regiments—the

43rd, 52nd, and the Rifle Corps—in the division. Napier halted these regiments just as they had forded the bitterly cold river on their way to the trenches. "Soldiers," he said, "I want 100 men from each regiment to form the storming party which is to lead the light division to-night. Those who will go with me come forward!" Instantly there was a rush forward of the whole division, and Napier had to take his 300 men out of a tumult of nearly 1500 candidates. He formed them into three companies, under Captains Ferguson, Jones, and Mitchell. Gurwood, of the 52nd, led the forlorn hope, consisting of twenty-five men and two sergeants. Wellington himself came to the trench and showed Napier and Colborne, through the gloom of the early night, the exact position of the breach. A staff-officer looking on, said, "Your men are not loaded. Why don't you make them load?"

Napier replied, "If we don't do the business with the bayonet we shall not do it all. I shall not load."

"Let him alone," said Wellington; "let him go his own way."

Picton had adopted the same grim policy with the third division. As each regiment passed him, filing into the trenches, his injunction was, "No powder! We'll do the thing with the *could* iron."

A party of Portuguese carrying bags filled with grass were to run with the storming party and throw the bags into the ditch, as the leap was too deep for the men. But the Portuguese hesitated, the tumult of the attack on the great breach suddenly broke on the night, and the forlorn hope went running up, leaped into the ditch a depth of eleven feet, and clambered up the steep slope beyond, while Napier with his stormers came with a run behind them.

In the dark for a moment the breach was lost, but found again, and up the steep quarry of broken stone the attack swept. About two-thirds of the way up Napier's arm was smashed by a grape-shot, and he fell. His men, checked for a moment, lifted their muskets to the gap above them, whence the French were firing vehemently, and forgetting their pieces were unloaded, snapped them. "Push on with the bayonet, men!" shouted Napier, as he lay bleeding. The officers leaped to the front, the men with a stern shout followed; they were crushed to a front of not more than three or four. They had to climb without firing a shot in reply up to the muzzles of the French muskets.

But nothing could stop the men of the light division. A 24-pounder was placed across the narrow gap in the ramparts; the stormers leaped over it, and the 43rd and 52nd, coming up in sections abreast, followed. The 43rd wheeled to the right towards the great breach, the 52nd to the left, sweeping the ramparts as they went.

Meanwhile the other two attacks had broken into the town; but at the great breach the dreadful fight still raged, until the 43rd, coming swiftly along the ramparts, and brushing all opposition aside, took the defence in the rear. The British there had, as a matter of fact, at that exact moment pierced the French defence. The two guns that scourged the breach had wrought deadly havoc amongst the stormers, and a sergeant and two privates of the 88th—Irishmen all, and whose names deserve to be preserved—Brazel, Kelly, and Swan—laid down their firelocks that they might climb more lightly, and, armed only with their bayonets, forced themselves through the embrasure amongst the French gunners. They were furiously attacked, and Swan's arm was hewed off by a sabre stroke; but they stopped the service of the gun, slew five or six of the French gunners, and held the post until the men of the 5th, climbing behind them, broke into the battery.

So Ciudad Rodrigo was won, and its governor surrendered his sword to the youthful lieutenant leading the forlorn hope of the light division, who, with smoke-blackened face, torn uniform, and staggering from a dreadful wound, still kept at the head of his men.

In the eleven days of the siege Wellington lost 1300 men and officers, out of whom 650 men and 60 officers were struck down on the slopes of the breaches. Two notable soldiers died in the attack—Craufurd, the famous leader of the light division, as he brought his men up to the lesser breach; and Mackinnon, who commanded a brigade of the third division, at the great breach. Mackinnon was a gallant Highlander, a soldier of great promise, beloved by his men. His "Children," as he called them, followed him up the great breach till the bursting of a French mine destroyed all the leading files, including their general. Craufurd was buried in the lesser breach itself, and Mackinnon in the great breach—fitting graves for soldiers so gallant.

Alison says that with the rush of the English stormers up the breaches of Ciudad Rodrigo "began the fall of the French Empire." That siege, so fierce and brilliant, was, as a matter of fact, the first of that swift-following succession of strokes which drove the French in ruin out of Spain, and it coincided in point of time with the turn of the tide against Napoleon in Russia. Apart from all political results, however, it was a splendid feat of arms. The French found themselves almost unable to believe the evidence of their senses. "On the 16th," Marmont wrote to the Emperor, "the English batteries opened their fire at a great distance. On the 19th the place was taken by storm. There is something so *incomprehensible* in this that I allow myself no observations." Napoleon, however, relieved his feelings with some very emphatic observations. "The fall of Ciudad Rodrigo," he wrote to Marmont, "is an affront to you. Why had you not advices from it twice a week? What were you doing with the five divisions of Souham? It is a strange mode of carrying on war," &c. Unhappy Marmont!

Chapter 5

Badajos

It would be difficult to find in the whole history of war a more thrilling and heroic chapter than that which tells the story of the six great campaigns of the Peninsular war. This was, perhaps, the least selfish war of which history tells. It was not a war of aggrandisement or of conquest: it was waged to deliver not merely Spain, but the whole of Europe, from that military despotism with which the genius and ambition of Napoleon threatened to overwhelm the civilised world. And on what a scale Great Britain, when aroused, can fight, let the Peninsular war tell. At its close the fleets of Great Britain rode triumphant on every sea; and in the Peninsula between 1808-14 her land forces fought and won nineteen pitched battles, made or sustained ten fierce and bloody sieges, took four great fortresses, twice expelled the French from Portugal and once from Spain. Great Britain expended in these campaigns more than 100,000,000 pounds sterling on her own troops, besides subsidising the forces of Spain and Portugal. This "nation of shopkeepers" proved that when kindled to action it could wage war on a scale and in a fashion that might have moved the wonder of Alexander or of Caesar, and from motives, it may be added, too lofty for either Caesar or Alexander so much as to comprehend. It is worth while to tell afresh the story of some of the more picturesque incidents in that great strife.

On April 6, 1812, Badajos was stormed by Wellington; and the story forms one of the most tragical and splendid incidents in the military history of the world. Of "the night of horrors at Badajos," Napier says, "posterity can scarcely be expected to credit the tale." No tale, however, is better authenticated, or, as an example of what disciplined human valour is capable of achieving, better deserves to be told. Wellington was preparing for his great forward movement into Spain, the campaign which led to Salamanca, the battle in which "40,000 Frenchmen were beaten in forty minutes." As a preliminary he had to capture, under the vigilant eyes of Soult and Marmont, the two great border fortresses, Ciudad Rodrigo and Badajos. He had, to use Napier's phrase, "jumped with both feet" on the first-named fortress, and captured it in twelve days with a loss of 1200 men and 90 officers.

But Badajos was a still harder task. The city stands on a rocky ridge which forms the last spur of the Toledo range, and is of extraordinary strength. The river Rivillas falls almost at right angles into the Guadiana, and in the angle formed by their junction stands Badajos, oval in shape, girdled with elaborate defences, with the Guadiana 500 yards wide as its defence to the north, the Rivillas serving as a wet ditch to the east, and no less than five great fortified outposts—Saint Roque, Christoval, Picurina, Pardaleras, and a fortified bridge-head across the Guadiana—as the outer zone of its defences. Twice the English had already assailed Badajos, but assailed it in vain. It was now held by a garrison 5000 strong, under a soldier, General Phillipson, with a real genius for defence, and the utmost art had been employed in adding to its defences. On the other hand Wellington had no means of transport and no battery train, and had to make all his preparations under the keen-eyed vigilance of the French. Perhaps the strangest collection of artillery ever employed in a great siege was that which Wellington collected from every available quarter and used at Badajos. Of the fifty-two pieces, some dated from the days of Philip II. and the Spanish Armada, some were cast in the reign of Philip III., others in that of John IV. of Portugal, who reigned in 1640; there were 24-pounders of George II.'s day, and Russian naval guns; the bulk of the extraordinary medley being obsolete brass engines which required from seven to ten minutes to cool between each discharge.

Wellington, however, was strong in his own warlike genius and in the quality of the troops he commanded. He employed 18,000 men in the siege, and it may well be doubted whether—if we put the question of equipment aside—a more perfect fighting instrument than the force under his orders ever existed. The men were veterans, but the officers on the whole were young, so there was steadiness in the ranks and fire in the leading. Hill and Graham covered the siege, Picton and Barnard, Kempt and Colville led the assaults. The trenches were held by the third, fourth, and fifth divisions, and by the famous light division. Of the latter it has been said that the Macedonian phalanx of Alexander the Great, the Tenth Legion of Caesar, the famous Spanish infantry of Alva, or the iron soldiers who followed Cortes to Mexico, did not exceed it in warlike quality. Wellington's troops, too, had a personal grudge against Badajos, and had two defeats to avenge. Perhaps no siege in history, as a matter of fact, ever witnessed either more furious valour in the assault, or more of cool and skilled courage in the defence. The siege lasted exactly twenty days, and cost the besiegers 5000 men, or an average loss of 250 per day. It was waged throughout in stormy weather, with the rivers steadily rising, and the tempests perpetually blowing; yet the thunder of the attack never paused for an instant.

Wellington's engineers attacked the city at the eastern end of the oval, where the Rivillas served it as a gigantic wet ditch; and the Picurina, a fortified hill, ringed by a ditch fourteen feet deep, a rampart sixteen feet high, and a zone of mines, acted as an outwork. Wellington, curiously enough, believed in night attacks, a sure proof of his faith in the quality of the men he commanded; and on the eighth night of the siege, at nine o'clock, 500 men of the third division were suddenly flung on the Picurina. The fort broke into a ring of flame, by the light of which the dark figures of the stormers were seen leaping with fierce hardihood into the ditch and struggling madly up the ramparts, or tearing furiously at the palisades. But the defences were strong, and the assailants fell literally in scores. Napier tells how "the axemen of the light division, compassing the fort like prowling wolves," discovered the gate at the rear, and so broke into the fort. The engineer officer who led the attack declares that "the place would never have been taken had it not been for the coolness of these men" in absolutely walking round the fort to its rear, discovering the gate, and hewing it down under a tempest of bullets. The assault lasted an hour, and in that period, out of the 500 men who attacked, no less than 300, with 19 officers, were killed or wounded! Three men out of every five in the attacking force, that is, were disabled, and yet they won!

There followed twelve days of furious industry, of trenches pushed tirelessly forward through mud and wet, and of cannonading that only ceased when the guns grew too hot to be used. Captain MacCarthy, of the 50th Regiment, has left a curious little monograph on the siege, full of incidents, half tragic and half amusing, but which show the temper of Wellington's troops. Thus he tells how an engineer officer, when marking out the ground for a breaching-battery very near the wall, which was always lined with French soldiers in eager search of human targets, "used to challenge them to prove the perfection of their shooting by lifting up the skirts of his coat in defiance several times in the course of his survey; driving in his stakes and measuring his distances with great deliberation, and concluding by an extra shake of his coat-tails and an ironical bow before he stepped under shelter!"

On the night of April 6, Wellington determined to assault. No less than seven attacks were to be delivered. Two of them—on the bridge-head across the Guadiana and on the Pardaleras—were mere feints. But on the extreme right Picton with the third division was to cross the Rivillas and escalade the castle, whose walls rose time-stained and grim, from eighteen to twenty-four feet high. Leith with the fifth division was to attack the opposite or western extremity of the town, the bastion of St. Vincente, where the glacis was mined, the ditch deep, and the scarp thirty feet high. Against the actual breaches Colville and Andrew Barnard were to lead the light division and the fourth division, the former attacking the bastion of Santa Maria and the latter the Trinidad. The hour was fixed for ten o'clock, and the story of that night attack, as told in Napier's immortal prose, is one of the great battle-pictures of literature; and

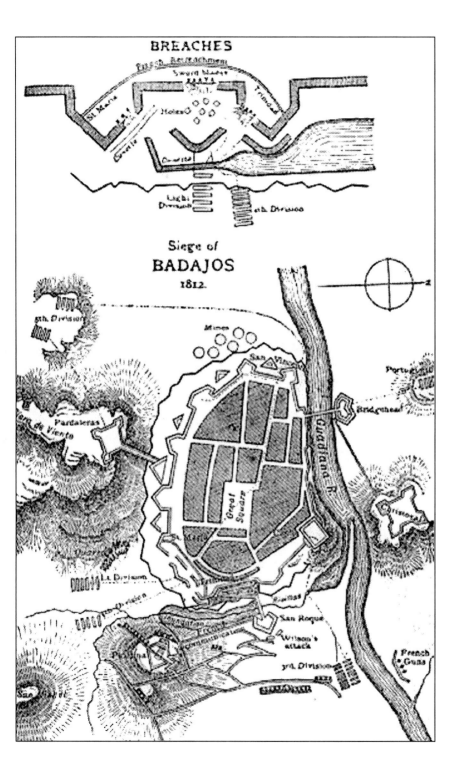

BREACHES

Siege of
BADAJOS
1812.

any one who tries to tell the tale will find himself slipping insensibly into Napier's cadences.

The night was black; a strange silence lay on rampart and trench, broken from time to time by the deep voices of the sentinels that proclaimed all was well in Badajos. "*Sentinelle garde à vous*," the cry of the sentinels, was translated by the British private as "All's well in Badahoo!" A lighted carcass thrown from the castle discovered Picton's men standing in ordered array, and compelled them to attack at once. MacCarthy, who acted as guide across the tangle of wet trenches and the narrow bridge that spanned the Rivillas, has left an amusing account of the scene. At one time Picton declared MacCarthy was leading them wrong, and, drawing his sword, swore he would cut him down. The column reached the trench, however, at the foot of the castle walls, and was instantly overwhelmed with the fire of the besieged. MacCarthy says we can only picture the scene by "supposing that all the stars, planets, and meteors of the firmament, with innumerable moons emitting smaller ones in their course, were descending on the heads of the besiegers." MacCarthy himself, a typical and gallant Irishman, addressed his general with the exultant remark, "Tis a glorious night, sir—a glorious night!" and, rushing forward to the head of the stormers, shouted, "Up with the ladders!" The five ladders were raised, the troops swarmed up, an officer leading, but the first files were at once crushed by cannon fire, and the ladders slipped into the angle of the abutments. "Dreadful their fall," records MacCarthy of the slaughtered stormers, "and appalling their appearance at daylight." One ladder remained, and, a private soldier leading, the eager redcoated crowd swarmed up it. The brave fellow leading was shot as soon as his head appeared above the parapet; but the next man to him—again a private—leaped over the parapet, and was followed quickly by others, and this thin stream of desperate men climbed singly, and in the teeth of the flashing musketry, up that solitary ladder, and carried the castle.

In the meanwhile the fourth and light divisions had flung themselves with cool and silent speed on the breaches. The storming party of each division leaped into the ditch. It was mined, the fuse was kindled, and the ditch, crowded with eager soldiery, became in a moment a sort of flaming crater, and the storming parties, 500 strong, were in one fierce explosion dashed to pieces. In the light of that dreadful flame the whole scene became visible—the black ramparts, crowded with dark figures and glittering arms, on the one side; on the other the red columns of the British, broad and deep, moving steadily forward like a stream of human lava. The light division stood at the brink of the smoking ditch for an instant, amazed at the sight. "Then," says Napier, "with a shout that matched even the sound of the explosion," they leaped into it and swarmed up to the breach. The fourth division came running up and descended with equal fury, but the ditch opposite the Trinidad was filled with water; the head of the division leaped into it, and, as Napier puts it, "about 100 of the fusiliers, the men of Albuera, perished there." The breaches were impassable. Across the top of the great slope of broken wall glittered a fringe of sword-blades, sharp-pointed, keen-edged on both sides, fixed in ponderous beams chained together and set deep in the ruins. For ten feet in front the ascent was covered with loose planks, studded with sharp iron points. Behind the glittering edge of sword-blades stood the solid ranks of the French, each man supplied with three muskets, and their fire scourged the British ranks like a tempest.

Hundreds had fallen, hundreds were still falling; but the British clung doggedly to the lower slopes, and every few minutes an officer would leap forward with a shout, a swarm of men would instantly follow him, and, like leaves blown by a whirlwind, they swept up the ascent. But under the incessant fire of the French the assailants melted away. One private reached the sword-blades, and actually thrust his head beneath them till his brains were beaten out, so desperate was his resolve to get into Badajos. The breach, as Napier describes it, "yawning and glittering with steel, resembled the mouth of a huge dragon belching forth smoke and flame." But for two hours, and until 2000 men had fallen, the stubborn British persisted in their attacks. Currie, of the 52nd, a cool and most daring soldier, found a narrow ramp beyond the Santa Maria breach only half-ruined; he forced his way back through the tumult and carnage to where Wellington stood watching the scene, obtained an unbroken battalion from the reserve, and led it towards the broken ramp. But his men were caught in the whirling madness of the ditch and swallowed up in the tumult. Nicholas, of the engineers, and Shaw, of the 43rd, with some fifty soldiers, actually climbed into the Santa Maria bastion, and from thence tried to force their way into the breach. Every man was shot down except Shaw, who stood alone on the bastion. "With inexpressible coolness he looked at his watch, said it was too late to carry the breaches," and then leaped down! The British could not penetrate the breach; but they would not retreat. They could only die where they stood. The buglers of the reserve were sent to the crest of the glacis to sound the retreat; the troops in the ditch would not believe the signal to be genuine, and struck their own buglers who attempted to repeat it. "Gathering in dark groups, and leaning on their muskets," says Napier, "they looked up in sullen desperation at Trinidad, while the enemy, stepping out on the ramparts, and aiming their shots by the light of fireballs, which they threw over, asked as their victims fell, 'Why they did not come into Badajos.'"

All this while, curiously enough, Picton was actually in Badajos, and held the castle securely, but made no attempt to clear the breach. On the extreme west of the town, however, at the bastion of San Vincente, the fifth division made an attack as desperate as that which was failing at the breaches. When the stormers actually reached the bastion, the Portuguese battalions, who formed part of the attack, dismayed by the tremendous fire which broke out on them, flung down their ladders and fled. The British, however, snatched the ladders up, forced the barrier, jumped into the ditch, and tried to climb the walls. These were thirty feet high, and the ladders were too short. A mine was sprung in the ditch under the soldiers' feet; beams of wood, stones, broken wagons, and live shells were poured upon their heads from above. Showers of grape from the flank swept the ditch.

The stubborn soldiers, however, discovered a low spot in the rampart, placed three ladders against it, and climbed with reckless valour. The first man was pushed up by his comrades; he, in turn, dragged others up, and the unconquerable British at length broke through and swept the bastion. The tumult still stormed and raged at the eastern breaches, where the men of the light and fourth division were dying sullenly, and the men of the fifth division marched at speed across the town to take the great eastern breach in the rear. The streets were empty, but the silent houses were bright with lamps. The men of the fifth pressed on; they captured mules carrying ammunition to the breaches, and the French, startled by the tramp of the fast-approaching column, and finding themselves taken in the rear, fled. The light and fourth divisions broke through the gap hitherto barred by flame and steel, and Badajos was won!

In that dreadful night assault the English lost 3500 men. "Let it be considered," says Napier, "that this frightful carnage took place in the space of less than a hundred yards square—that the slain died not all suddenly, nor by one manner of death—that some perished by steel, some by shot, some by water; that some were crushed and mangled by heavy weights, some trampled upon, some dashed to atoms by the fiery explosions—that for hours this destruction was endured without shrinking, and the town was won at last. Let these things be considered, and it must be admitted a British army bears with it an awful power. And false would it be to say the French were feeble men. The garrison stood and fought manfully and with good discipline, behaving worthily. Shame there was none on any side. Yet who shall do justice to the bravery of the British soldiers or the noble emulation of the officers? . . . No age, no nation, ever sent forth braver troops to battle than those who stormed Badajos."

Chapter 9

Salamanca

It was a French officer who condensed the story of Salamanca into the epigram that it was "the battle in which 40,000 men had been beaten in forty minutes." In an epigram, truth is usually sacrificed to picturesqueness, and this oft-quoted saying is in open quarrel with fact. The battle of Salamanca lasted, not forty minutes, but six hours. Yet, in dramatic quality, it is one of the most remarkable fights in modern history; and the tactics of the three or four weeks which preceded it the marches and counter-marches, the tangled manoeuvring, the swift thrust and swifter parry of two great masters in the art of war are almost as dramatic in their features as the battle itself.

Salamanca was fought on July 22, 1812. A little more than a month earlier on June 13 Wellington crossed the Portuguese border, and began the movement designed to drive the French out of Spain. It was a step of singular daring. Wellington had under his nominal command some 90,000 men, but they were widely scattered, composed of four different nationalities, were ill supplied and worse paid, and the number under his immediate command did not reach 50,000. The French, on the other hand, had 300,000 soldiers in Spain, of one blood and discipline, veterans in war, and led by generals trained in Napoleon's school and familiar with victory. Marmont, who directly confronted Wellington on the east, had 70,000 men under his standard; but the French system of "making war sustain war" of feeding an army, that is, by supplies taken from the enemy caused Marmont's troops to be widely scattered. Yet he had 52,000 present with the eagles. Marmont, too, had Madrid, strongly held by Napoleon's brother Joseph, behind him. Soult, to the south, held Andalusia with 56,000 men; Souham held the Asturias to the north with 38,000; Suchet had 76,000 men in Catalonia and Valencia.

Wellington's plan was to leap on Salamanca, capture it, and, if possible, crush or defeat Marmont before reinforcements could reach him. He thrust hard and fiercely, that is, at the French centre, and calculated that the thrust would draw the widely-scattered French armies from the extremities, and so, with one stroke, clear northern and southern Spain. In any case, the march to Salamanca and Madrid must bring Soult hurrying up from the south, as otherwise his communications with France would be cut off. To advance with 50,000 troops against forces numbering in all 300,000 was an act of signal hardihood. Wellington was thrusting his head, in brief, into the lion's mouth; and if, while engaged in deadly wrestle with Marmont at the centre, the French armies on either flank closed in upon him, he must be destroyed.

Wellington, however, measured with ice-clear intellect, and faced with ice-cool courage, the risks of this daring strategy, and made his historic dash at Salamanca. There were two circumstances in his favour. First, the French quite misread his strategy. Soult, on March 26, wrote he "was certain Wellington would march upon Andalusia to raise the siege of Cadiz." But Wellington, with more subtle strategy, proposed to raise the siege of Cadiz by striking at Salamanca! The other circumstance in Wellington's favour was the total want of concert betwixt the French generals. Napoleon, whose genius alone could control their fierce jealousies of each other, was far off in Russia. Joseph lacked the skill and daring of a great soldier. His more famous brother had put the crown of Spain upon his head, but he could not put within that head the brains necessary to sustain it; and his generals were loyal neither to him nor to each other. Napoleon himself attributed the loss of Salamanca to the "vanity "of Marmont, eager rather to win personal fame than to serve France. But that same flame of restless and selfish vanity burned in the breasts of all the French marshals. They cared more to outshine each other than even to beat the common enemy.

Wellington reached Salamanca on June 17, and Marmont, who could assemble only 25,000 troops, fell back before 'him. But he left Salamanca strongly fortified. No less than thirteen convents and twenty-two colleges, it was said, had been pulled down to yield material for the French forts; and these were heavily armed with artillery, while Wellington had only four heavy guns and three 24-pounders, and a very scanty supply of ammunition for even these. Marmont reckoned that the forts would hold out for at least fifteen days; and in less than that time he would be heavily reinforced from Madrid and from the north, and could then advance and crush Wellington. Wellington's attack, however, was fierce. The men who had stormed Badajos and Ciudad Rodrigo were not to be denied at Salamanca, and the forts would have fallen in five days, but that ammunition failed and gave the garrison a brief respite.

Marmont found he must do something to divert the fierceness with which the British pressed on his forts. He was a gallant soldier, a fine tactician, full of French Man, and of a half-scornful eagerness to overthrow the mere "sepoy general" opposed to him, and drive the British into the sea; and with a force of 30,000 he advanced in very tempestuous fashion against the force covering the attacked forts. Wellington knew that a barren victory would be hardly less disastrous than a defeat, and was determined to fight only when he could destroy his enemy. He was content with barring Marmont's advance, day after day, by positions skilfully taken up, until on June 29 the forts surrendered. Marmont then fell back with shrewish wrath to the Duero, holding the northern bank of it from Tordesillas to Toro a distance of less than fourteen miles there to await the reinforcements pressing to join him. Wellington followed him in the expectation that either the difficulties of gathering supplies would compel Marmont to fall back, or his impatient and eager genius would make him attempt some rash stroke.

Marmont, however, was a tactician of the first order. His troops were hardy and quick of foot. The country, a series of open rolling downs seamed with shallow rivers, lent itself to rapid movements, and was perfectly familiar to him; and he commenced a series of swift movements in which, again and again, he out-marched and out-generalled Wellington. His aim, in brief, was to march round Wellington's flank, and strike at the Ciudad Rodrigo road on his rear, which formed his only line of retreat to Portugal. And the feints and movements on his part to accomplish, and on Wellington's part to prevent, this, form, one of the most brilliant chapters of tactics in the history of war.

The movements of the armies resembled the quick and gleaming thrusts and parries of two accomplished fencers engaged in fierce and close duel; or, to vary the figure, the armies circled round and dashed at each other with breathless attack and recoil, like two contending hawks in mid-air, swooping on each other in airy curves that grow ever closer. There is no space here to tell the story of this struggle, which lasted more than a week, and in which the weapons were not so much bayonet and sabre, as the brains of the general and the legs of the soldier. But some of the picturesque incidents yielded by that struggle in generalship are worth describing.

Marmont, on July 16, made a show of crossing the Duero at Toro, and so marching past Wellington's left to Salamanca. Wellington moved to his left to block this road, but yet, as a precaution, left the fourth and light divisions and Anson's cavalry, under Sir Stapleton Cotton, on the Trabancos, so as to guard against any advance past his right from Tordesillas. As soon as Marmont saw the bulk of the British forces drawn to his right, he countermarched his troops, pressed on at the utmost speed back to Tordesillas, crossed the Duero there without pause, and came rushing down past Wellington's right towards Salamanca. Some of his men actually marched forty miles, some fifty, without a halt!

It was a brilliant stroke of generalship, and on the evening of the 17th, Cotton, with two divisions and some cavalry, was, without support, in the presence of the whole French army. Cotton had the obstinate courage that grows yet more stubborn in actual combat, characteristic of his race, and he clung to his position. In the deep folds of the treeless downs the full strength of the French was hidden, and Cotton, with cheerful confidence, drove back the skirmishers as they crossed the stream. But the columns of the French became denser, their fire heavier; and soon the deep sound of heavy guns was added to the sharp crackle of musketry.

It was early morning, and the black masses of powder-smoke mingled with the light mists rising from the river. Here is a vivid battle-picture, taken from Napier:

> The cannonade became heavy, and the spectacle surprisingly beautiful, for the lighter smoke and mist, mingling and curling in fantastic pillars, formed a huge and glittering dome tinged with many colours by the rising sun; and through the grosser vapour below the restless horsemen were seen or lost, as the fume thickened from the rapid play of the artillery, while the bluff head of land beyond the Trabancos, covered with French troops, appeared by an optical deception close at hand, dilated to the size of a mountain, and crowned with gigantic soldiers, who were continually breaking off and sliding down into the fight. Suddenly a dismounted English cavalry officer stalked from the midst of the smoke towards the line of infantry; his gait was peculiarly rigid, and he appeared to hold a bloody handkerchief to his heart; but that which seemed a cloth was a broad and dreadful wound; a bullet had entirely effaced the flesh from his left shoulder and breast, and carried away part of his ribs, his heart was bared, and its movement plainly discerned. It was a piteous and yet a noble sight; for his countenance, though ghastly, was firm, his step scarcely indicated weakness, and his voice never faltered. This unyielding man's name was Williams; he died a short distance from the field

of battle it was said, in the arms of his son, a youth of fourteen, who had followed his father to the Peninsula in hopes of obtaining a commission, for they were not in affluent circumstances.

By seven o'clock Wellington, accompanied by Beresford, drawn by the sound of the firing, had reached the scene of the conflict, and was almost at once in great personal peril.

A couple of squadrons of French cavalry, gallantly led by their officer, swept down the farther bank of the river, splashed through the current, and galloped up the steep slope beyond. As they reached the crest, disordered and breathless, they found themselves confronted with a squadron of British dragoons. The Frenchmen were heavy cavalry, splendidly mounted, hi gay uniform, with high fur caps. Their officer halted his men within a hundred yards of the British cavalry, thrown out in skirmishing order, held his sword high in air, and, with a shout of *"Vive l'Empereur! En avant, Francois!"* dashed on the British, who were carried away in a moment by the rush of the heavier horses of the French. The whole mass, French and British, struggling together, and smiting furiously at each other, went tumbling down the reverse slope.

In the valley below were two guns, covered by some infantry pickets and another squadron of light cavalry; and without a pause the French officer rode at these, his men following, and swept through them like a whirlwind, the artillerymen stooping, with heads bent, spurring their horses to save their guns, while the Frenchmen slashed at them with their sabres. Wellington and Beresford were caught in the middle; and Maxwell tells how he saw the British general as he crossed the ford "with his straight sword drawn, at full speed, and smiling." At this moment a squadron of heavy British dragoons charged the furious French swordsmen, and the latter were destroyed almost to a man; but "their invincible leader," says Napier, "assaulted by three enemies at once, struck one dead from his horse, and, with surprising exertions, saved himself from the other two, though they rode hewing at him from each side for a quarter of a mile."

Meanwhile Marmont, having discovered how small was the force opposed to him, crossed the Trabancos, and pushed on straight for the Guarena. If he could throw himself across it before the British, Wellington would be cut off from Salamanca.

Ten miles of dusty soil had to be crossed under a blazing sun and at high speed. The troops that could march fastest would win. And, urged by their officers to the utmost exertions, the rival columns pressed on. It was one of the strangest scenes ever witnessed in war, and only Napier's resonant prose can do justice to it:

> The British retired in three columns, the light division being between the fifth division and the French, close to the latter, the cavalry on the flanks and rear. The air was extremely sultry, the dust rose in clouds, and the close order of the troops was rendered very oppressive by a *siroc* wind; but where the light division marched the military spectacle was strange and grand. Hostile columns of infantry, only half musket-shot from each other, were marching impetuously towards a common goal, the officers on each side pointing forward with then swords, or touching their caps and waving their hands in courtesy, while the German cavalry, huge men on huge horses, rode between in a close compact body, as if to prevent a collision: at

times the loud tones of command to hasten the march were heard passing from the front to the rear on both sides, and now and then the rush of French bullets came sweeping over the columns, whose violent pace was continually accelerated.

Thus moving for ten miles, yet keeping the most perfect order, both parties approached the Guarena, and the enemy, seeing the light division, although more in their power than the others, was yet outstripping them in the march, increased the fire of their guns and menaced an attack with infantry: the German cavalry instantly drew close round, the column plunged suddenly into a hollow dip of ground on the left, and ten minutes after the head of the division was in the stream of the Guarena between Osmo and Castrillo. The fifth division entered it at the same time higher up on the left, and the fourth division passed on the right. The soldiers of the light division, tormented with thirst, yet long used to their enemy's mode of warfare, drank as they marched; those of the fifth division, less experienced, stopped a few moments, and on the instant forty French guns, gathering on the heights above, sent a tempest of bullets amongst them. So nicely timed was the operation.

Maxwell describes the scene as the river was reached. "A buzz," he says, "ran through the ranks that water was at hand; and the soldiers were impelled forward with eyes staring and mouths open; and when within fifty yards of the stream a general rush was made."

The French general had accomplished much. He had crossed a great river, surprised Wellington's right, and driven it back for ten miles. Nevertheless, a glance at the map shows how Wellington had thwarted the attempt to sweep past his flank and get between him and Salamanca. Marmont's troops, too, had been marching for two days and nights, and were exhausted, and a brief pause followed. The two great hosts bivouacked on the opposite slopes of a narrow valley, and the outposts were placed so near each other that, to quote Maxwell, "the fixed sentinels almost received the secret whispers of each other's watch!"

On the morning of the 20th, Marmont was moving again. His light-footed battalions, while the stars were yet burning in the Spanish night skies, were pushing past Wellington's right up the Guarena. Parallel lines of hills, with a very narrow and shallow valley betwixt, run curving to the south-west towards the Tormes, on which river stands Salamanca; and along the crest of the outer range Marmont pushed at fiercest speed. On the inner ridge, and within easy musket-shot, marched the British, the eager columns trying to head each other. Wherever the ground favoured the movement, the guns on either side wheeled round, and smote the hostile flank opposite them with grape and round shot. But the dusty panting soldiers, with sloping muskets and shoulders thrown forward, never halted; while, to quote Napier, "the officers, like gallant gentlemen, who bore no malice and knew no fear, made their military recognitions, and the horsemen on each side watched with eager eyes for an opening to charge." At one point the swiftly moving lines, for a moment, so to speak, jostled, and two dust-covered brigades on either side clashed fiercely together. The British, however a brigade of the fourth division swung round, poured in a deadly volley, charged home with bayonet, dashed their opponents into mere fragments, then wheeled back, and pressed on their scarcely interrupted march.

In this day's operations, however, Marmont won. He outmarched and outflanked the British, and when night fell his dusty and exhausted soldiers held the ford of Huerta on the Tonnes. He had nothing to do but to keep that position till his reinforcements reached him, then Salamanca and Wellington's line of retreat to Portugal lay under his stroke. The night set in wild and stormy. Rain fell with tropical violence. The hill-slopes were slippery with a thousand rills; a furious thunderstorm broke over the valley, where the tired armies, in great confusion, were trying to take up their positions. The peals of thunder were so deep and echoing, that a whole troop of British cavalry horses, familiar with the roar of artillery, broke loose in terror, and galloped riderless into the French camp. Hundreds of frightened horses, too, dashed through the British lines, and were mistaken for charges of French cavalry. Never was a wilder scene. But, through it all, the soldiers of the immortal light division "were seen by the fiery gleams to step from the river to the bank, and pursue their march, amid this astounding turmoil, in close and beautiful order, defying alike the storm and the enemy."

Wellington recognised that in this strife of tactics Marmont had won; but he clung with iron tenacity to his position, in the hope that the Frenchman, instead of waiting till his reinforcements came up and made a battle hopeless, might attempt a rash stroke on his own account. But he wrote a letter to the Spanish general, Castanos, saying he must retreat. The orderly carrying the letter was captured by the French, and his despatch, falling into Marmont's hands, tempted him to his doom. The French insisted afterwards that this letter was a subtle *ruse de guerre* on Wellington's part. It was written to trick Marmont, not to inform Castafios;

and its capture was part of the trick. The letter, it is quite true, tempted Marmont to make the rash stroke which ruined him; but it also exactly expressed Wellington's purpose. Retreat was the only course possible to him if Marmont stood on his defence till his reinforcements came up.

A glance at the map shows that the Tormes forms a great loop north of Salamanca. Marmont, on the night of July 18, had seized the ford at Huerta, at the crown of the loop, and could move down either bank of the river to Salamanca. Wellington entrenched his third division on the right bank of the river, opposite the ford of Santa Marta, to bar Marmont's advance, but with the bulk of his army crossed the river, and took up a position perpendicular to its course, his extreme right touching, but not occupying, one of a pair of rugged and isolated hills, called the Arapiles. He thus covered Salamanca against Marmont's advance from Huerta, on the left bank of the river.

The two wearied armies watched each other for a day and a half; but Wellington had learnt that Marmont's reinforcements from the north would reach him on July 22 or 23, and the British general decided that he must retreat. Still, he hung on, hoping for some chance of a dramatic stroke, and this suddenly offered itself. Marmont had crossed to the left bank of the Tormes, and, on the morning of the 22nd, he suddenly made a leap at the outer of the two hills we have named. The hills were about 500 yards apart, and the British, quick to see the French movement, made a dash at the hill near them. The French, vehement and swift footed, reached the hill on the side first, seized it, and dashed on to the sister hill, which the slower, but more stubborn, British had half climbed. There was a struggle, fierce, short, and bloody; but at its close the French and the British held their respective hills, and these two savage splinters of rock formed, so to speak, the menacing heads, from which two great armies threatened each other. But the capture of the French Arapiles gave Marmont a great advantage. It made his right unassailable, and he could swing round from the hill as from a pivot, and strike at the Ciudad Rodrigo road, along which Wellington must retreat. Wellington met the situation thus created by using the English Arapiles as a fixed point, and swinging round his army till his right rested on Aldea Tejada. What had been his first line facing Huerta, thus became his rear, and the army now looked eastward to meet the wheel of the French left.

The long summer day crept on, both armies grimly watching each other. Wellington had resolved to fall back as soon as night came. Marmont, on his part, was fretted to fever by the dread that Wellington would slip out of his hands before his reinforcements came up. The English commissariat wagons were already on the road to Ciudad Rodrigo, and the dust, rising high in the sky, made Marmont believe that Wellington was actually in retreat; and, taking fire at that thought, he launched his left, consisting of two divisions under Maucune, with fifty guns and some light cavalry, along a ridge of low hills which ran in a curve past Wellington's right towards Salamanca. The two armies, in fact, occupied the opposing crests of an oval-shaped amphitheatre, whose axis, from east to west, was about two miles long, the transverse axis, from north to south, being about a mile and a half; and to the northern tip of this natural amphitheatre the two Arapiles acted, so to speak, as gateposts.

Marmont's left was now in movement, and its march quickly created a steadily widening gap in the French line

of battle. Wellington's keen and soldierly eye instantly detected the flaw in his enemy's tactics. The French left wing was entirely separated from the centre. The fault was flagrant, and, in Napier's terse phrase, Wellington "fixed it with the stroke of a thunderbolt." Croker, in his journal, relates a conversation at Strathfield Saye, many years afterwards, in which Alava, while Wellington was present and listened, and smiled at the story, drew a realistic sketch of the manner in which Marmont's unlucky move was detected by the British general:

He (Wellington) had been very busy all the morning, and had not thought of breakfast, and the staff had grown very hungry; at last, however, there was a pause (I think he said about two) near a farmyard surrounded by a wall, where a kind of breakfast was spread on the ground, and the staff alighted and fell to. While they were eating, the Duke rode into the enclosure; he refused to alight, and advised them to make haste; he seemed anxious and on the look-out. At last they persuaded him to take a bit of bread and the leg of a cold roast fowl, which he was eating without knife from his fingers, when suddenly they saw him throw the leg of the fowl far away over his shoulder, and gallop out of the yard, calling to them to follow him. The fact is, he had been waiting to have the French sighted at a certain gap in the hills, and that was to be the signal of a long-meditated and long-suspended attack. 'I knew,' said Alava, with grave drollery, 'that something *very serious* was about to happen when an article so precious as the leg of a roast fowl was thus thrown away!

Wellington, in brief, waited coolly till Marmont's faulty movement was developed past remedy; then he made his terrible counter-stroke. He fixed Marmont's right to its ground by making a dash at the French Arapiles; he smote the head of Maucune's columns with the third division brought up at the double from Aldea Tejada, and, at the same moment, he launched at their flank the fifth division. How swift and dramatic was the development of Wellington's attack is best told in Napier's vivid sentences:

> A few orders issued from his lips like the incantations of a wizard, and suddenly the dark mass of troops which covered the English Arapiles, as if possessed by some mighty spirit, rushed violently down the interior slope of the mountain and entered the great basin, amidst a storm of bullets which seemed to shear away the whole surface of the earth over which they moved.
>
> The fifth division instantly formed on the right of the fourth, connecting the latter with Bradford's Portuguese, who hastened forward at the same time from the right of the army; and the heavy cavalry, galloping up on the right of Bradford, closed this front of battle.

The first and most decisive blow of the great fight was struck by the third division. These were Picton's men; but that brave soldier was absent through sickness, and the division was under the command of Pakenham, Wellington's brother-in-law, a soldier of excellent fighting quality. Wellington gave his orders in person to Pakenham.

"Do you see those fellows on the hill, Pakenham?" he said, pointing to where Maucune's columns were now showing. "Move on with your division, and drive them to the d—!"

Pakenham saluted, and there are two versions of his reply. "I will, my lord, by G—," is the reply put in his mouth by Robinson in his *Life of Picton*. Napier's version of the reply is, "Yes, if you will give me a grasp of that all-conquering hand."

The first version is needlessly profane, the second is tumid and un-British; but about the intelligence and fire with which Pakenham carried out his orders there is no doubt. Wellington himself watched the division as it deployed into column and moved fiercely to attack, an attack which was described by an eye-witness as "not only the most spirited, but the most perfect thing of its kind ever seen."

"Did you ever see a man," said Wellington to his staff, "who understood his orders better than Pakenham?"

Pakenham's columns, as they drew near the French, swung into line, the companies bringing forward their right shoulders at a run as they marched, and with bent heads and levelled bayonets, but not yet firing a shot, pressed sternly on the French, who, expecting to look down on the Ciudad Rodrigo road crowded with a retreating enemy, instead suddenly found themselves threatened by swiftly moving lines of steady infantry, glittering from end to end with, shining bayonets at the charge. But the French were hardy veterans, and broke instantly into an angry fire of musketry. Their guns, too, swung round and poured a storm of grape on the steady British lines.

These never wavered or halted. The gaps in their front were filled instantly. On they came, their disciplined tread sounding louder and nearer, till they burst into dreadful and fast-following volleys, and the French were swept away as with the blast of a whirlwind. The French officers were gallant men, and did desperate acts to keep their men steady. The colonel of a French regiment, for example, snatched a musket from a grenadier, ran forward a few yards, and shot Major Murphy, in command of the 88th or Connaught Rangers, who was in advance of his men. One of the 88th in return shot the Frenchman dead; but Murphy's horse galloped wildly across the front of the regiment, dragging his dead rider, whose foot was entangled in the stirrup, with him.

The sight kindled the 88th to madness. The line began to sway forward with the eager fury of the men; and Pakenham, who rode near, shouted to Wallace, who commanded the brigade, to "let them loose." The word of command ran down the line, repeated from officer to officer; the bayonets fell as with one impulse to the level; and, "let loose," the men with a sudden shout dashed at the enemy. Amid the smoke of the French line a single officer could be seen lingering to fire the last gun. But, crushed as though smitten with a tempest of aerolites, the French columns broke in hopeless flight. The French cavalry rode at the flanks of the victorious British, and for a few minutes horsemen and footmen were mingled in desperate fight. The French cavalry, however, was quickly driven off; and, steadily moving on its path, the third division struck with its fire the second line of the French, while the fifth division was pouring its volleys at the same moment into the French flank.

Then came one of the most memorable cavalry charges on record. The heavy brigade the 3rd and 4th Dragoons, and the 5th Dragoon Guards under Le Marchant, and Anson's light cavalry, found the opportunity of a decisive attack. The squadrons were launched at speed:

While Pakenham, bearing onward with a conquering violence, was closing on their flank, and the fifth division advancing with a storm of fire on their front, the interval between the two attacks was suddenly filled with a whirling cloud of dust, moving swiftly forward and carrying within its womb the trampling sound of a charging multitude. As it passed the left of the third division, Le Marchant's heavy horsemen, flanked by Anson's light cavalry, broke forth from it at full speed, and the next instant 1200 French infantry, though formed in several lines, were trampled down with a terrible clamour and disturbance. Bewildered and blinded, they cast away their arms and ran through the openings of the British squadrons, stooping and demanding quarter; while the dragoons, big men on big horses, rode onwards, smiting with their long glittering swords in uncontrollable power; and the third division followed at speed, shouting as the French masses fell in succession before the dreadful charge.

The charging cavalry struck first the 66th Regiment of the French, formed in a sort of column of half battalions, thus presenting six successive lines which broke into a heavy musketry fire as the cavalry dashed on the front. Over these the British horsemen rode at a gallop, simply trampling them out of existence. A second battalion of six hundred was served in the same fashion. Onward swept the eager horsemen. By this time the open trees, under which the British cavalry was galloping, grew closer, and the front of the charging line was greatly broken. A solid French brigade, which stood in the shelter of the trees, poured a stream of fire into the galloping squadrons, and scores of saddles were emptied. Yet the stubborn horsemen kept on, and crushed to fragments this, the third body they had encountered; and Lord Edward Somerset, with a single squadron seeing beyond him a battery of five guns, pushed on his attack and captured, them. This memorable charge destroyed Maucune's three divisions, as a military body, and captured five guns and 2000 prisoners. But Le Marchant himself, perhaps the best cavalry leader in the British army, had fallen, and the three regiments of the heavy brigade at nightfall could muster only three squadrons.

One curious incident marked the cavalry charge. Captain Mackie of the 88th, who acted as aide-de-camp to Wallace, the commander of the brigade, was, about .this stage of the battle, reported as "missing." No one had seen him fall, but he had disappeared. Some half-hour later he reappeared through the smoke from the enemy's front, covered with dust and blood, his horse stumbling from fatigue, and nothing left of his sword but the hilt. As the English cavalry swept past the 88th, on their great charge, Mackie's Highland blood had kindled to flame; he galloped to the flank of the cavalry, shared in the tumult and rapture of their mad ride, and, when it was over, returned to his regiment hi the fashion we have described.

It was five o'clock when Pakenham attacked, and before six o'clock Marmont had been carried disabled off the field; his successor, Bonet, was wounded; the French left had been destroyed as a military body, and had fallen back in tumultuous and disorderly retreat. But two circumstances for a brief space changed the fortunes of the conflict, and seemed to make the final issue doubtful. Clausel, who assumed command of the French when Bonet fell, was a fine soldier, stubborn of courage and fertile in resource. He not only rallied the broken left and shaken centre, but, with the instinct of a valiant soldier, he attempted a daring counterstroke on Wellington's left; and chance for a moment seemed to offer him a golden opportunity. Wellington assailed the French Arapiles with Pack's Portuguese brigade. Pack's men were 2000 strong, and Pack himself was "a fighting general" of fine courage. The hill, too, was held by a single French battalion, and the success of the attack seemed assured. And yet it failed! Pack led his men up within thirty yards of the summit in solid column; then over the crest and round the flank of the hill the French came in a furious charge, pushed home with fiery valour; and the Portuguese broke. "There was a cloud of smoke, a shout, a stream of fire, and the side of the hill was covered with the killed, the wounded, and the flying Portuguese."

French valour in this attack was heightened by contempt of the Portuguese, and Portuguese courage, it may be added, was rebuked by a lurking consciousness of inferiority to the French. But it is not easy to excuse 2000 men for permitting themselves to be routed by less than 600.

French valour is always most dangerous when the imagination of victory gleams like a flame in it. The 4th division of the British had at that moment reached the edge of the southern ridge. Pack's defeat exposed their flank, and Clausel, seizing the critical moment, smote hard on their front with two strong unbroken regiments, and the British were driven in tumult and confusion, but fighting desperately, down the hill. Cole, in command of the division, fell badly wounded. Beresford brought up a Portuguese brigade to restore the fight, but the brigade was carried away, and Beresford himself was disabled. The French heavy cavalry was coming on to the attack, and the moment was critical. Wellington, riding quickly to the scene, brought up Clinton's division, which had not yet fired a shot, and the fury and thunder of the fight grew still deeper.

Night was falling. The dry grass on the slope where the hostile lines were exchanging close and deadly volleys, and making furious rushes with the bayonet, took fire, and ran in crackling flames over the bodies of the wounded, and under the trampling feet of the combatants. But the stubborn close-fighting valour of the 6th overbore the fiery daring of the French, and the changing current of battle set finally in favour of the British. The whole volume of the French retreat flowed in wild far-reaching tumult along the Alba de Tonnes road. Still its rear-guard, however, clinging to every vantage of ground, covered the retreat with sullen and desperate courage, and Foy in command of it showed fine skill. The fragments of Maucune's division held the last defensible ridge on the edge of the forest through which the French retreat, with loud clamour, was flowing. It was night, black and moonless; and Clinton, scornful of tactics and flank movements, led his division straight up the hill. To those who watched the fight from a little distance, the eddying fortunes of the attack and the defence were written in ever-changing characters of fire on the hill-slopes.

In the darkness of the night the fire showed from afar how the battle went. On the English side a sheet of flame was seen, sometimes advancing with an even front, sometimes pricking forth in spear-heads, now falling back in waving lines, anon darting upwards in one vast pyramid, the apex of which often approached yet never gained the actual summit of the mountain; but the French musketry, rapid as lightning, sparkled along the brow of the height with unvarying fullness, and with what destructive effects the dark gaps and changing shapes of the adverse fire showed too plainly: meanwhile Pakenham turned the left, Foy glided into the forest, and, Maucune's task being then completed, the effulgent crest of the ridge became black and silent, and the whole French army vanished as it were in the darkness.

The French must cross the Tormes in their flight at Alba de Tormes or at Huerta. Wellington had placed a Spanish garrison at the first, and he pushed on to the second with the light division. If he could seize that, the French army must surrender or be destroyed. The Spanish garrison, however, had abandoned Alba de Tormes without reporting the circumstance to Wellington; and the French army crossed the Tormes at that point in safety, and pushed on their retreat with such speed that, on the day after the fight, Clausel was forty miles from Salamanca. Wellington overtook the French rear-guard with his cavalry a little before noon on the 23rd, and launched the heavy German dragoons and Anson's light horsemen at them. Then ensued a cavalry exploit of singular brilliancy. Anson's troopers broke the French cavalry; but the Germans, riding fast, with narrow front, up the valley, discovered some solid squares of infantry on the slope above them. The left squadron of the regiment instantly swung round and rode at the nearest square. The two front ranks, kneeling, presented a double row of deadly steel; and over their heads, the French infantry, standing four deep, poured a stream of fire into the swiftly moving mass of men and horses before them. The Germans, however, gallantly led, pushed their charge up to the very points of the bayonets. A horse struck by a bullet stumbled forward on to the square, and broke for a moment its solid order, and the Germans big men on huge horses swept through the gap, and in an instant the battalion was cut down or trampled out of existence.

Meanwhile the second squadron, taking fire at the exploit of the squadron next to it, also swung round and rode fiercely at the second French square. Its fire was angry and damaging; but its ranks had been shaken by the spectacle of the destruction which had just ridden over the square below it. One or two French infantrymen ran from their places, and in an instant the tempest of galloping horses and furious swordsmen broke over the square. A third square, according to one version, was in like manner destroyed by the triumphant cavalry; but the remaining square stood firm and succeeded in covering the French retreat. The charge was a memorable feat. Three squares were broken and 1400 prisoners captured. Yet a great price was paid for this triumph.

> The hill of La Serna offered a frightful spectacle of the power of the musket that queen of weapons and the track of the Germans was marked by their huge bodies. In several places man and horse had died simultaneously, and so suddenly that, falling together on their sides, they appeared still alive, the horse's legs stretched out as in movement, the rider's feet in the stirrup, his bridle in hand, the sword raised to strike, and the large hat fastened under the chin, giving to the grim but undistorted countenance a supernatural and terrible expression.'

Salamanca is one of the great battles of modern history. The French army was practically destroyed as a military body. "I never saw an army receive such a beating," wrote Wellington, the least exaggerative of men. But the immediate results of Salamanca were its least important consequences. It destroyed the splendid prestige of the French. It delivered Madrid. It raised the siege of Cadiz. It rescued Andalusia and Castile from the French occupation. Napoleon heard the tidings of the defeat the night before Borodino, and it filled him with fury and with reason. He could henceforth hope for no reinforcements from Spain; he must drain his strength, indeed, when he most needed it, to feed the war there. "The Spanish ulcer," said Napoleon long afterwards, "destroyed me." But it was Salamanca that made the Spanish ulcer incurable.

CHAPTER 10

San Sebastian

A rugged breach in a long line of parapeted wall, at whose base a river creeps sluggishly to the sea. The breach is black with drifting smoke, and crowded with red-coated soldiers. Many lie dead under the feet of their comrades; many have crept, with streaming wounds, to either flank. The faces of the soldiers yet on the breach are black with powder, fierce with the passion of battle. From the walls above them, from a line of higher parapets that sweeps round at right angles, and commands the breach, a hundred streams of fire converge on the swaying mass of red-coated soldiers. They are dying in hundreds. Suddenly, from beyond the stream, and from the iron lips of fifty great guns, a tempest of shot roars above the heads of the British, soldiers, and sweeps the edge of the wall where the fiercely triumphant Frenchmen have defied for two separate hours the utmost valour of the British. For twenty minutes the British guns maintain that overwhelming fire above the heads of their own troops the most brilliant bit of artillery practice on record. The French parapets are swept as with a besom of flame, the traverses are wrecked, the lines of steadfast infantry are rent to fragments. Then, with a flame of passion scarcely less fierce than the flame of the bellowing guns, the British stormers swept in one red wave over the blackened parapets, and

San Sebastian is won! This is the scene which, through the long afternoon of August 31, 1813, makes the siege of San Sebastian one of the most picturesque in military history.

Three great sieges those of Ciudad Rodrigo, of Badajos, and of San Sebastian stand out like flaming beacons in the stern landscape of the Peninsular war. Each siege has its special characteristic. That of Ciudad Rodrigo was a swift and brilliant stroke of arms; it resembles, indeed, nothing so much as the flash of a glittering blade in the hands of a great swordsman. That of Badajos is notable for the masterful and furious daring with which the great breach was carried. The capture of San Sebastian is not marked by the swift brilliancy of Ciudad Rodrigo, nor yet by the tempestuous and half-scornful valour of Badajos. Its characteristic consists of the sullen daring, with a note of wrath running through it, which marked the temper of the soldiers. It is the most bloody and tragical of all the Peninsular sieges. Wellington's sieges in the Peninsula, it may be added, are not shining examples of scientific warfare. In each of them he was short of guns, of warlike material, and, above all, of time. In each he had to make the blood of his soldiers compensate for the blunders of his engineers, and the well-nigh incredible neglect, or equally incredible folly, of the War Office authorities in England. It was, perhaps, the sullen consciousness on the part of the private soldiers, that they had to pay in life and limb for stupidity, or neglect, in the administration of the war, which explains the exasperated temper in the ranks with which the siege of San Sebastian was conducted, and the blast of licence and cruelty with which it was closed.

San Sebastian, while the French held Central Spain, was

a neglected third-rate fortress, with foul wells, dismantled batteries, and practically no garrison. But the great defeat of Vittoria made this sandy peninsula, with its steep rocky tip, a place of the first importance to both armies. The French clung to it, as it would be a thorn in Wellington's flank if he advanced through the passes of the Pyrenees. Wellington coveted it, as its harbour would be a new base of supply for him, and he dared not leave unsubdued what might be easily turned into a strong place of arms, as he pushed on the track of the defeated French through the wild mountain denies which led to France.

San Sebastian resembles a lion's head thrust out from the coast of the Bay of Biscay, just where the spurs of the Pyrenees run down to the sea. The "neck "of the lion is a flat sandy isthmus, some 350 yards wide; the lion's head looks to the north, the bay is under its chin to the west; on the east flows into the sea in a wide shallow tidal channel the river Urumea. The seaward tip of the lion's head is a rocky cone, some 400 feet high, called Monte Orgullo, crowned by the castle of La Mota. Across the sandy isthmus ran a high solid curtain with a huge horn-work, shaped like the point of an arrow, at its centre. Betwixt this wall and the base of Monte Orgullo stretched the town, having a population of something like 10,000 people. A line of ramparts ran along the eastern face of the town, betwixt the curtain across the neck of the isthmus and Monte Orgullo. The Urumea washed the foot of this rampart, and the frowning heights of Monte Orgullo commanded with their batteries the whole town.

Fortune gave to the French, in the person of General Rey, a commander for San Sebastian with a singular genius for defensive war. Rey, indeed, in personal appearance was quite unheroic. Fraser, who was second in command of the British artillery at the siege, met Rey after the surrender, and describes him as "a great fat man," in appearance resembling rather a pacific and heavy-bottomed Dutch burgher, than one of the most brilliant soldiers of the Napoleonic wars. Rey was not present at Vittoria; he left the day before the battle in command of a great convoy. The convoy passed on to France, but Rey, with his escort, entered San Sebastian, and set himself with stern energy, and the genius of a fine soldier, to prepare for the siege which he knew to be inevitable. Part of the wreck of Vittoria a few days afterwards flowed in wild tumult and confusion into the town; but Rey, with great resolution, swept the town of non-combatants, armed all his batteries, cleared out his trenches and wells, turned the convent of San Bartolomeo, some 600 yards in advance of the curtain crossing the isthmus, into a strong place of arms; and, with all the art of a veteran soldier, set himself to hold San Sebastian against all comers. He had a garrison of some 3000 men; and 10,000 British and Spanish troops, under Sir Thomas Graham, the "hero of Barossa," one of Wellington's most trusted lieutenants, were moving down the slope of the Pyrenees to besiege him.

The Frenchman, however, had many things in his favour. San Sebastian lent itself easily to a stubborn defence. San Bartolomeo formed a strong outwork to the south; behind this, on the main road which crossed the narrow neck of the isthmus rose a great circular redoubt, formed of casks, and flanked by ruined houses, strongly held. These in turn were covered by the strong rampart which crossed the isthmus, with a powerful horn-work rising high in its centre. Thus, no less than three lines of defence had to be broken through before the town was reached. The town itself must be carried by obstinate street-fighting, while Monte Orgullo, with the stroke of its batteries, covered the whole field of combat, and could be held independently after the town itself had been carried.

The happiest feature for the French was the fact that they had practically an open sea base, and were in daily communication with France. It is an amazing fact that, eight years after Trafalgar, and while Great Britain was absolutely mistress of the sea, Wellington could not secure any adequate naval assistance in the siege of San Sebastian. A single British frigate, the *Surveillante*, represented all the naval help the Admiralty could afford. Wellington's transports were captured almost daily by French privateers. The French garrison was perpetually fed by supplies sent directly from France. Vainly Wellington appealed to the Admiralty for ships. "Since Great Britain had been a naval power," he wrote bitterly, "a British army had never before been left in such a situation at a most important moment."

Wellington's genius, however, was essentially practical, as he wrote to Lord Bathurst:

> If the navy of Great Britain cannot afford more than one frigate and a few brigs and cutters, fit, and used only, to carry despatches, to co-operate with this army in the siege of a maritime place, the possession of which before the bad season commences is important to the army as well as to the navy, I must be satisfied, and do the best I can without such assistance. ... We have been obliged to use the harbour boats of Passages, navigated by women, in landing the ordnance and stores, because there was no naval force to supply us with the assistance we require in boats.

Wellington, in brief, in this siege of a hostile port, had to leave the aid of British ships out of his calculation.

But the aid the French derived from the open sea was simply past calculation. Boats came nightly to the garrison from Bayonne, bringing engineers, artillerymen, supplies of every kind, with news from the outside world, promises from Soult of immediate relief, and decorations, badges of honour, and crosses of the Legion of Honour in profusion to the soldiers who, from day to day, distinguished themselves in the siege. In this way the imagination of the besieged French was fed, as well as their material wants supplied. And the sense that a way of escape to the rear was open, that France was watching their defence, and that every act of valour brought an immediate reward in the shape of some "decoration," or of promotion, bred such a spirit of daring and enthusiasm in the garrison that, says Maxwell who was actually a prisoner in San Sebastian: "I believe the garrison, individually or collectively, would not have hesitated attempting any enterprise, however difficult or dangerous."

The principles of war are changeless, and Wellington's engineers adopted the very plan of attack employed by the Duke of Berwick, who besieged San Sebastian in 1719. Strong batteries were erected on the Chofres sandhills, to smite with their fire the comparatively weak eastern wall across the stream of the Urumea. Approaches were simultaneously to be pushed along the isthmus, so as to take in flank the wall which the breaching batteries were smiting in front, and to smash the defences by which the breach, when made, would be guarded. The plan was able, and if it had been carried out the siege would never have attained what Napier calls its "mournful celebrity." Wellington, however, was guarding the passes against Soult, and left the conduct of the siege to Graham; and Graham allowed the eager spirits about him to over-ride what their impatience regarded as the too formal approaches of the engineers. They inverted, in a word, Vauban's well-known maxim, "Never attempt to carry anything at a siege by open force which may be gained by art and labour." The British leaders at San Sebastian scorned to postpone the bayonet to the spade or the linstock! So there became visible in the conduct of the siege that "raw haste" which is something more than "half-sister to delay."

Batteries were marked out on the night of July 10, 1813; by the morning of the 14th the guns were thundering across the front of the isthmus on San Bartolomeo; but not till the 20th did the breaching batteries across the Urumea begin to smite with their fire the eastern wall of the town. Even at this early stage in the siege the British began to feel the strength of the defence. Fraser writes in his diary on July 19: "The enemy has some good head in the fortress; we must feel for it. He fires and takes his measures with judgment."

Nothing could well surpass the energy with which the siege was pushed. The great breaching battery had ten guns in action, and in fifteen and a half hours of daylight the fire from these averaged 350 rounds a gun; "such a rate of firing," says Jones in his *Journal*, "was probably never equalled at any siege." The, sustained fury of the fire on both sides, indeed, quickly affected the guns in use. The guns fired from the fortress, for example, gave the appearance of two explosions when discharged; the vent of the gun, in a word, being so enlarged that the flash from it was almost as clear as that from the muzzle; while in the English batteries, Jones records, that "some of the vents of the guns were so much enlarged that a moderate-sized finger might be put into them."

The attacks on the two faces of the defence were of course part of one scheme, and should have been pushed on with a wise balance of energy. But Graham, apparently, found it impossible to keep the too eager spirits of his force in check; and, as a result, the attack on the isthmus was urged on with fiery energy, and without any regard to the operations against the eastern front of the town. By the 17th, San Bartolomeo was almost knocked out of shape; and though the batteries had not yet opened fire against the eastern front it was impossible to cool the impatience of the attack on the southern face. On the 17th the convent was assaulted. From the engineering point of view the attack was premature; but it was a brilliant and picturesque feat of arms.

The convent stood upon a steep ridge, and was open to the fire of both besiegers and besieged. From the batteries on the Chofres sandhills, and from the rocky height of Monte Orgullo, the French and British alike eagerly watched the fierce struggle for the convent. No less than sixty guns indeed concentrated their fire on the building while the attack raged the French guns smiting the assailants, the British guns trying to crush the defenders. At ten o'clock the storming party in two columns came over the crest of the hill which looked down on the convent. It consisted of Wilson's Portuguese, supported by the light company of the 9th British, and three companies of the Royals. Colin Campbell, afterwards Lord Clyde, led the men of the 9th. The Portuguese came on slowly, and the four companies of the British pushed forward with impatient eagerness, carried the redoubt, jumped over the convent wall, and thrust the French fiercely out. The French clung stubbornly to the houses which stretched beyond the convent towards the town, but the other companies of the 9th coming up with great resolution the French were still thrust back, while the cheers of the British troops watching the struggle from the farther bank of the Urumea, could be heard above the tumult of the fight. The reckless daring of the British carried them too far; they tried to carry the great circular redoubt, which stood betwixt the convent and the town. Musket and bayonet were vain, however, to carry a work so strong, and the too eager soldiers were driven back with sharp loss.

The convent was at once turned into batteries against the southern front of the defence, and the eastern wall of the town began to crumble under the stroke of the guns from the Chofres hills. A parallel was carried by the British across the neck of the isthmus, and in its course laid bare an ancient aqueduct, a great drain four feet high and three feet wide. A young officer, Reid, of the Engineers, crept up this drain; he found it ran for 230 yards towards the curtain across the isthmus, and ended in a door in the very counter-scarp itself. A space of eight feet at the end of the aqueduct was stopped with sandbags, and thirty barrels of gunpowder were lodged against it, thus forming a globe of compression. This was to be fired at the moment of the assault, and it was hoped would blow, as through a tube, enough rubbish over the counterscarp as would fill the ditch of the horn-work, and thus make a way for the stormers.

Meanwhile the eastern wall crumbled fast under the fire of the batteries across the river. On July 23, the great breach was declared practicable. A day was spent in making a second breach a little to the north of the first, and the assault was fixed for the next morning. When the troops, in the grey dawn, however, were waiting in the trenches for the signal to attack, the houses behind the great breach broke into flames, and the attack was postponed to the next day a very unhappy circumstance.

The proposed attack was in violation of the simplest rules of engineering. A breach was to be stormed, in a word, before the defences which covered it with their fire had been mastered. Rey had made these defences exceedingly powerful. The horn-work, or cavalier, at the centre of the southern front, rose fifteen feet above the other defences, and swept the breach with the fire of its guns. A tower on either side of the breach raked it with a flanking fire; the houses immediately behind the breach were strongly defended. The British, too, could only attack by leaping from the eastern extremity of the trench which crossed the isthmus, and advancing at the double for 300 yards along the slippery strand left at low water betwixt the Urumea and the undestroyed wall of the town, till they reached the breach. For those 300 yards they were under a flank fire of musketry from the walls; while Rey had piled the parapet with live shells to be rolled down on the struggling British. The attack was directed by Wellington to take place "in fair daylight," so that the batteries across the Urumea might keep down the fire of the defenders. Unfortunately, the signal for the attack was given whilst the night was still black, and the batteries on the Chofres hills were unable to open fire on the defenders, except at the risk of smiting their own troops.

The attacking force consisted of 2000 men of the 5th division: Fraser led a battalion of the Royal Scots against the great breach; the 38th, under Greville, was to attack the more distant breach; the 9th, under Cameron, supported the Royals, while the forlorn hope consisted of twenty men of the light company of the 9th, and the light company of the Royals, with a ladder party, under Colin Campbell. The opening from the trench was too narrow, and the formation of the troops was broken at the very outset. The 300 yards to be traversed was slippery with weeds and rocks, and broken by deep pools of water, while at every step a fierce fire scourged the flank of the broken soldiers. The assault, in a word, from its very first step became the rush of a mob, instead of a disciplined and orderly attack. The globe of compression in the aqueduct, already described, was indeed fired with a blast that tilled the surrounding hills with its echoes, and the surprise of it drove the French for a moment from their defences.

Fraser and the principal engineering officer, Harry Jones, led eagerly on to the great breach, followed by the soldiers immediately about them; but the mass of the attacking party halted in the dark to fire at a gap in the wall which they mistook for the breach. In a few minutes the halt filled the narrow interval betwixt the wall and the river with a struggling crowd of soldiers, aflame with the passion of battle, but without order or leaders. Colin Campbell, with a few men, struggled past the flank of the crowd, and climbed the great breach, and a few disconnected parties followed up the rough slope. These gallant men reached the broken crest of the breach, but the French had meanwhile recovered from their surprise. Those who reached the crest of the breach saw below them a deep black gulf, beyond which, in a curve of fire, was a wall of flaming houses, and from every quarter a tempest of shot swept the rugged edge of broken stone on which they stood. Fraser of the Royal Scots, leaped down the farther side of the breach, reached the flaming houses, and died there. Greville, Cameron, Campbell, and other gallant officers broke through the tumult of the crowd, climbed the breach, and fell on its crest. Twice Campbell ascended, and twice he was wounded. Meanwhile, the mass of British soldiers below, with the black river now filling again with the returning tide and climbing the rocks fast on one side, and the hostile wall, with its perpetual hail of bullets on the other side, swayed to and fro with sullen shouts and angry answering fire of musketry. But, with military cohesion destroyed, and scourged on both flank and front by the fire of the French, the mass crumbled into clusters, and surging backwards, slowly regained the trenches. When day broke, Fraser of the Artillery, watching from the batteries beyond the Urumea, thought that nothing more than a false attack had taken place; till, in the clearer daylight he could see the rough slope of the great breach mottled with red spots, the fallen bodies of officers and men.

This bloody and ill-managed assault resulted in a loss to the British, in killed, wounded, or prisoners, of forty-four officers and nearly 500 men. Perhaps the best account of the attack and its failure, is to be found in a private letter written by Colin Campbell at the time, and published in his life:

It was dark, as you know, when ordered to advance. All before me went willingly enough forward, but in a very straggling order, arising, in the first instance, from the order of formation previous to attack being extended the whole length of the parallel in a front of fours, which it (the parallel) would admit of by packing when halted, but was not of sufficient width for troops to maintain that front when in movement.

We thus debouched from the mouth of the opening made from the parallel, which was not quite so wide as the latter, in twos and threes. The space we had to traverse between this opening and the breach some 300 yards was very rough, and broken by large pieces of rocks, which the falling tide had left wet and exceedingly slippery, sufficient in itself to have loosened and disordered an original dense formation; and the heavy and uninterrupted fire to which they were opposed in advance, increased this evil these different causes combining to make our advance look more like one of individuals than that of a well-organised and disciplined military body.

On arriving within some thirty or forty yards of the demi-bastion on the left of the main front, I found a check. There appeared to be a crowd of some 200 men immediately before me, opposite the front of this work those in front of this body returning a fire directed at them from the parapet above, and which was sweeping them down in great numbers, and also from an entrenchment which the enemy had thrown across the main ditch, about a yard or two retired from the opening into it. I observed at the same time a heavy firing at the breach; and as the larger portion of the right wing appeared to be collected, as I have described, opposite the demi-bastion, it was very manifest that those who had gone forward to the breach were not only weak in numbers for the struggle they had to encounter, but it was apparent they were also unsupported. I endeavoured with the head of my detachment to aid some of their own officers in urging and pushing forward this halted body. They had commenced firing, and there was no moving them. Failing in this, I proposed to Lieutenant Clarke, who was in command of the light company of the Royals, to lead past the right of these people, in the hope that, seeing us passing them, they might possibly cease firing and follow. I had scarcely made this proposition when this fine young man was killed; and several of my own (9th) detachment, as also many of the light company Royals, were here killed and wounded. In passing this body with the few of my own people and most of the light company Royals, some might have come away, but the bulk remained. Their halting there (opposite the demi-bastion) thus formed a sort of stopping-place between the trenches and the breach, as the men came forward from the former on their way to the latter. . . . On arriving at the breach, I observed the whole lower parts thickly strewed with killed and wounded. There were a few individual officers and men spread on the face of the breach, but nothing more. These were cheering, and gallantly opposing themselves to the close and destructive fire directed at them from the round tower and other defences on each flank of the breach, and to a profusion of hand-grenades which were constantly rolling down. In going up I passed Jones of the Engineers, who was wounded; and on gaining the top I was shot through the right hip, and tumbled to the bottom. The breach, though quite accessible, was steep, particularly towards the top, so that all those who were struck on the upper part of it rolled down, as in my own case, to the bottom. Finding, on rising up, that I was not disabled from moving, and observing two officers of the Royals, who were exerting themselves to lead some of their men from under the line-wall near to the breach, I went to assist their endeavours, and again went up the breach with them, when I was shot through the inside part of the left thigh.

About the time of my receiving my second hit, Captain Archimbeau of the Royals arrived near the bottom of the breach, bringing with him some eighty or ninety men, cheering and encouraging them forward in a very brave manner through all the interruptions that were offered to his advance by the explosion of the many hand-grenades that were dropped upon them from the top of the wall, and the wounded men retiring in the line of his advance (the narrow space between the river and the bottom of the wall). Seeing, however, that whatever previous efforts had been made had been unsuccessful that there was no body of men nor support near to him, while all the defences of and around the breach were fully occupied and alive with fire, and the party with him quite unequal in itself seeing, also, the many discouraging circumstances under which the attempt would have to be made, of forcing its way through, such opposition he ordered his party to retire, receiving, when speaking to me, a shot which broke his arm. I came back with him and his party, and on my way met the 38th, whose advance became interrupted by the wounded and others of the Royals returning.

The attack had thus failed; and in the British batteries the supply of ammunition was exhausted; Soult was coming fiercely on through the passes of the Pyrenees, and Wellington had no choice but to turn the siege into a blockade till fresh supplies arrived from England. Thirty days had been spent in open trenches, and thirty days of blockade followed; days, as far as Wellington, who was covering the siege, was concerned, of desperate and bloody fighting. But Soult's gallant host, at the close of these operations, was sweeping, a broken mass, in wild tumult back to France, with a loss, in killed, wounded, and prisoners, of not less than 20,000 men. Then Wellington resumed the siege. On August 19, a battering train arrived from England; on the 23rd came a second battering train; but, with a touch of administrative stupidity delightfully characteristic, ammunition for only a single day's consumption was sent out with the guns!

On the morning of the 26th, the batteries opened in thunder on the doomed city. No less than 114 guns were in action at once. For four days that tempest of fire was maintained. By August 30 two wide breaches gaped in the eastern wall, the fire of the place was almost silenced, three mines had been run from the southern attack towards the curtain crossing the isthmus, and everything seemed ready for the final assault. The gallant French commandant, however, had spent the thirty days of the blockade in perfecting his defences; and, with a wise prevision of the difficulties before them, Fraser records in his *Diary* on August 22: "This St. Sebastian is destined to be a thorn in our sides, or a feather in our caps." At this stage the "thorn" was more visible than the "feather"!

Rey, the French commandant, did not hope to maintain an equal duel with the furious British batteries; his plan was to make assault on the breach hopeless. He constructed immediately behind the great breach an interior rampart, 15 feet high, with outstanding bastions. The apparent breach, therefore, was, in effect, a death trap. On reaching its crest the storming party would find before it a huge pit, from 20 to 35 feet deep, its bottom strewn with every sort of impediment; and beyond it a new and unbroken rampart, loopholed for musket-fire, with traverses at either extremity. A mine charged with 1 2 cwt. of powder was driven beneath the slope along which the stormers must come; two other mines were designed to blow down part of the sea-wall on .the British columns as they passed along it to the attack. Never, in fact, was a more desperate task than that of carrying San Sebastian. And it is to be noted that the engineering blunder which made the first attack a failure was repeated. The defences that covered the breach were left undestroyed.

On the night of August 29, a false attack was made on the breach, in order to tempt the besieged to spring their mines, and show the direction and scale of the fire they had prepared for the assaulting column. Lieutenant Macadam, of the 9th, was ordered, with a handful of men nearest him, to make a pretended attack on the breach. Macadam leaped out of the trench, seventeen men of the Royals at the word of command followed him; and, running forward, reached the foot of the great breach, and in extended order, with loud shouts, and discharging their muskets, proceeded to mount it. They were, of course, flinging their lives away. If the trick had succeeded, these brave men, by their very success, would have been blown into fragments. The French, however, kept their coolness, and shot these brave fellows down, one by one, their leader alone regaining the trenches.

Meanwhile Wellington, dissatisfied with the conduct of his men in the first attack, called for fifty volunteers from each of the fifteen regiments in the 1st, 4th, and light divisions; "men" the appeal ran, "who could show other troops how to mount a breach." That stinging phrase was felt by the gallant men of the 5th division like the stroke of a whip; but the response in the other divisions was eager, and even tumultuous. Here is a picturesque little passage from the *Private Journal* of Larpent:

> There was nothing but confusion in the two divisions here last night (the light and 4th), from the eagerness of the officers to volunteer, and the difficulty of determining who were to be refused and who allowed to go and run their heads into a hole in the wall, full of fire and danger! Major Napier was here quite in misery, because, though he had volunteered first, Lieutenant-colonel Hunt of the 52nd, his superior officer, insisted on his right to go. The latter said that Napier had been in the breach at Badajoz, and he had a fair claim to go now. So it is among the subalterns; ten have volunteered where two are to be accepted. Hunt, being lieutenant-colonel, has nothing but honour to look to; as to promotion, he is past that. The men say that they don't know what they are to do, but they are ready to go anywhere.

The *Historical Record* of the 52nd says that when Wellington's appeal reached that regiment . . . .

> . . . .entire companies volunteered, and the captains had a difficult task in selecting the men most fit for such an undertaking, without hurting the feelings of the others; in many cases lots were resorted to to settle the claims of those gallant fellows who contended for the honour of upholding the fame of their regiment.

When the order was communicated to the 4th division, and volunteers were invited to step to the front, the whole division moved forward!

Leith, however, who commanded the 5th division, was much aggrieved at the slight put upon his men, and he placed the 750 volunteers who were to "show other troops how to mount a breach" in support, and gave the men of the 5th division the post of honour. The men of that division, indeed, were so exasperated with the slight put upon them that there was some risk of them firing on the volunteers themselves, instead of on the French!

The assault was fixed for 11 o'clock on the morning of August 31. Robinson's brigade was formed in two columns. One was to storm the eastern end of the curtain that crossed the isthmus, the other was to assail the great breach; Bradford's Portuguese were to cross the river and assault the smaller and more northerly breach.

The morning broke gloomy and black. A dense mist drifted down from the high valleys of the Pyrenees, and girdled San Sebastian with a shroud of grey vapour, so dense that the besieging batteries could not fire. As the day advanced, however, the fog lifted, and a tempest of shot was poured for more than two hours on the defences of the city. Eleven o'clock struck; the batteries suddenly ceased. Robinson's men leaped from their trench, and a river of scarlet uniforms swept towards the breach. It was known that heavy mines were in the path of the column; but twelve men led by a sergeant ran forward at speed, and leaped upon the covered way to cut the fuse by which the mine was to be exploded. Startled by their rush, the French hurriedly fired the mine. The sergeant and his brave band were instantly destroyed, and the great sea-wall was thrown, with a terrific crash, upon the flank of the advancing column, crushing some forty men beneath it. Had it been fired some five minutes later it would have slain hundreds. As it was it did not arrest the attack for a moment. McGuire, of the 4th, who led the forlorn hope, "conspicuous," says Napier, "from his long white plume, his fine figure, and his swiftness, bounded far ahead of his men in all the pride of youthful strength and courage. But at the foot of the great breach he fell dead, and the stormers went sweeping, like a dark surge, over his body."

On pressed the stormers. Their array was broken by the slippery rocks, over which they stumbled as they charged, and by the fire which scourged them from the summit of the wall on their left. But they reached the breach, swept up it without a pause, and gained its narrow crest. They found themselves on the edge of a gulf, barred at its further edge by a frowning rampart, from which flashed incessantly the flame of the French muskets; while from every side a storm of bullets swept over them. The flow of the eager soldiers up the breach was constant, but there was no living in the deadly fire that played on the crest. The attack on the half bastion of St. John was equally obstinate and bloody, and equally ineffective. The breach was flanked by a traverse held by French grenadiers; it was scourged by guns from every angle. The British could not force their way; they would not yield, and they fell fast and thick. Still the attack was fed by fresh troops; but both breaches were barred as by a sword of flame.

The volunteers from the other divisions had been held back with difficulty so far, and were now calling out to know "why they had been brought there if they were not to lead the assault." They were at last let loose; and, to quote Napier:

. . . . went like a whirlwind to the breaches, and again the crowded masses swarmed up the face of the ruins; but reaching the crest line they came down again like a falling wall. Crowd after crowd were seen to mount, to totter, and to sink. The deadly French fire was unabated. The smoke floated away, and the crest of the breach bore no living man.

This dreadful struggle, with its tumult and bloodshed, the passionate heroism of the attack, the unyielding valour of the defence, lasted for two hours. The lesser breach had been assailed by the Portuguese, under Snodgrass, with no better fortune.

Graham had watched the long struggle from a battery on the farther side of the Urumea. He saw that valour could accomplish no more on the bloodstained breaches, and he resorted to an expedient of singular daring. He turned fifty heavy pieces on the parapet of the high curtain whose fire barred the breach. The British soldiers clung to the slope of the breach only a few feet below the level at which the British guns were firing; but the British gunners, after five days' continuous firing, knew the range precisely, and the practice was perfect. A tempest of shot swept along the edge of the high curtain, broke down its traverses, and slew the exultant French infantry that lined it. For thirty minutes, with this whip of flame, the ramparts of the curtain were scourged; then, suddenly, a series of explosions ran along the crest of the parapet. All the stores of powder-barrels, live shells, hand-grenades, &c., piled there took fire. The curtain was lost for a moment to sight in a cloud of smoke through which ran the shock, and the wavering flame of the explosion. Three hundred French grenadiers were destroyed in a moment; then through the smoke, on the staggering French came the British stormers, mad with the passion of combat, and the rage bred of the long slaughter they had suffered. The French colours on the horn-work were plucked down by Lieutenant Gathin of the 11th. The French clung to their broken defences with amazing valour, but were thrust back fiercely and triumphantly by the British; and, after five hours of dreadful combat at the walls, the whirlwind of battle swept into the town.

Fraser, who watched the assault from a battery across the river, describes the spectacle of the assault as "awful." He took pencil notes of the assault, from moment to moment, part of which is reproduced here. It gives the great struggle, so to speak, as in the present tense.

Minutes taken during the assault of San Sebastian:

It begins (5 minutes before 11)! They reach the top of the breach. A mine springs, but behind them! All seems well. They reach the top and halt if they are supported it will do. Mirador and St. Elmo do not fire. Men run too much to old breach too little to junction of demi-bastion and curtain.

11.35: Much firing. Troops do not advance. Bugles sound advance. Head of Portuguese column cross to left in detached columns, men pass creek up to knees; advance nobly at double quick; fourteen taken back wounded with grape, about fifty more turn back; main body advance. Lieutenant Gathin, 11th Regiment, acting engineer, runs to the Portuguese to storm with them.

11.45: The Portuguese get across but with great loss. At the breaches all is stationary. Another reinforcement runs from trenches to breach.

11.50: More reinforcements from trenches to breach. Noon: Much grape in all directions from the enemy's batteries. Breaches are filled. . . .

12.10 p.m.: Fire slackens on all sides. At a quarter-past eleven a letter was brought across the water by Private O'Neil, of the 4th (Portuguese run from the breach), from Lord Wellington, asking Sir Thomas Graham if he can spare Bradford's brigade, as Soult comes on in force.

12.15: Advancing from breach of retired wall; smoke prevents clear view. Lodgement apparently secure. Two more mines blown up on curtain.

12.25: Ditch toward low communication filled with troops. More reinforcements from trenches to breach.

12.30: Troops again try the end of curtain; our own shots strike close over their heads. The place will be taken! Our men run from the curtain. . . .

12.40: Men going down from the old breach into the town. It will do; they wave their hats from the *terre pleine* of the curtain. Another reinforcement from trenches. Our men fire from right of right round tower. This bounds our ground to right.

1.00: More reinforcements from trenches. This duty is well performed, whoever may direct it. Men enter the town, principally by the end of old breach next round tower. One man of 1st Guards runs alone to the part of the parapet, twenty yards to the right of the right tower, and a sergeant and a few Portuguese by right breach of all. They gain it by getting on the old foundation of Marshal Berwick's wall. The enemy lines the stockade. The enemy runs from the rampart behind that stockade. All goes well.

1.10: Two of our shots go through the stockade; the enemy abandons it. One brave French officer and two men alone remain; they too are gone.

1.15: Enemy still holds end of the curtain next the cavalier; he should be forced at that point. The gun at St. Elmo fires.

1.20: And again it must be silenced. Very heavy fire of musketry in the town. Horn-work decidedly ours.

1.25: The gun at St. Elmo more and more troublesome. Firing in the town continues and increases. Few men comparatively on breaches; chiefly in hollow of retired wall between end of curtain and left tower; they are now entering the town. The flag was struck on the castle when the assault began.

1.35: More reinforcements to breach from trenches. No fire or men to be seen on trenches. Wind very high; sand blows and destroys the view. Many prisoners brought into trenches from the town. Tide has begun to flow.

1.45: Heavy musketry in the town. Our bugles sound the advance in all parts of the town. Our men are pulling prisoners out by the breach. The enemy retire.

1.55: Fire in town slackens.

2.00: Marshal Beresford and Sir Thomas Graham come to the battery. Town seems again on fire near the right breach.

2.05: News of Sir Richard Fletcher's death!

2.15: Firing in town continues, but is decreasing. Gabions carrying into town from trenches.

2.48: Great fire and smoke in centre of town near the square. Two mines explode in the town. The enemy still hold a church and the left part of the town.

3.00: Mules with ammunition going from trenches to town. Three fires in the town. Between rain, and smoke, and black sky, it is very dark.

3.30: Great fire in the town; as dark as it is generally at half-past six. Nothing of the town to be seen from excessive smoke.

A thunderstorm which had been gathering round the crest of the shaggy summits of the nearest mountains now broke upon the city; and perhaps a wilder scene than that which was now presented has seldom been witnessed. The town was in flames. The streets were filled with the crash of musketry volleys, the oaths and shouts of contending men; while overhead rolled the deep voice of thunder, and from the black sky the incessant lightning leaped. The French commandant fell back, fighting with sullen valour, to Monte Orgullo, from which he was only to be driven by a new siege; but the town itself had fallen. Yet at what a price had this victory been won! The slaughter at the breaches was dreadful. Of the 750 volunteers who were "to show other troops how to mount a breach" every second man had fallen. The total loss of the assault, in killed and wounded, amounted to 2000 men. Many officers of rank fell. The troops, it may be added, when they broke into the town, got completely out of hand; and a shadow which blackens the fame of the splendid and obstinate valour by which the breaches were carried is cast by the scenes of cruelty and license which followed the assault. The men who swept the streets of the unhappy city as that night fell were drunk with the long madness of the fight, and Graham had no fresh troops at hand which he could march into the town to enforce order.

Fraser, it may be added, gives a realistic picture of the town as seen after the attack:

> I have been in the town, and over that part of it which the flames or the enemy will permit to be visited. The scene is dreadful; no words can convey half the horrors which strike the eye at every step. Heaps of dead in every corner; English, French, and Portuguese lying wounded on each other; with such resolution did one side attack and the other defend. The town is not plundered; it is sacked. Rapine has done her work, nothing is left. I had occasion, in going to General Hay, to go into several houses, some had been elegantly furnished. All was ruin; rich hangings, women's apparel, children's clothes, all scattered in utter confusion. The very few inhabitants I saw said nothing. They were fixed in stupid horror, and seemed to gaze with indifference at all around them, hardly moving when the crash of a fallen house made our men run away. The hospitals present a shocking sight: friends and enemies lying together, all equally neglected.

Napier says that "the place was won by accident" the *accident* being the explosion of the powder-barrels and grenades along the high curtain. But that accident was due to Graham's happy use of the British artillery in the very crisis of the assault. Jones in his *Journal*, says that:

. . . . on inspecting the defences it was found that the tremendous enfilade fire on the high curtain, though it lasted only twenty minutes, had dismounted every gun but two. Many of these pieces had their muzzles shot away, and the artillerymen lay mutilated at their stations. The parapet was thickly strewed with headless bodies.

But the terrible effects of that cannonade only suggest how gross was the blunder of not making this use of the batteries earlier. It belongs to the alphabet of the engineer's art that the fire which guards a breach should be mastered before the breach itself is assailed. A great siege, however, like a great battle, is usually a catalogue of blunders. In the story of San Sebastian these blunders are thrown into even blacker relief by the dazzling splendour of the courage shown by both men and officers in that great struggle on the bloodstained breach, and through the blackened streets of the city the French had defended with so much skill and courage.

CHAPTER 6

Mountain Combats

The brilliant and heroic combats on the Nive belong to the later stages of the Pyrenean campaign; and here, as on the Bidassoa, Soult had all the advantages of position. He had a fortified camp and a great fortress as his base; excellent roads linked the whole of his positions together; he held the interior lines, and could reach any point in the zone of operations in less time than his great opponent. Wellington, on the other hand, had almost every possible disadvantage. The weather was bitter; incessant rains fell; he had to operate on both sides of a dangerous river; the roads were mere ribbons of tenacious clay, in which the infantry sank to mid-leg, the guns to their axles, the cavalry sometimes to their saddle-girths. Moreover, Wellington's Spanish troops had the sufferings and outrages of a dozen campaigns to avenge, and when they found themselves on French soil the temptations to plunder and murder were irresistible. Wellington would not maintain war by plunder, and, as he found he could not restrain his Spaniards, he despatched the whole body, 25,000 strong, back to Spain. It was a great deed. It violated all military canons, for by it Wellington divided his army in the presence of the enemy. It involved, too, a rare sacrifice of personal ambition. "If I had 20,000 Spaniards, paid and fed," he wrote to Lord

Bathurst, "I should have Bayonne. If I had 40,000 I do not know where I should stop. Now I have both the 20,000 and the 40,000, . . . but if they plunder they will ruin all." Wellington was great enough to sacrifice both military rules and personal ambition to humanity. He was wise enough, too, to know that a policy which outrages humanity in the long-run means disaster.

Wellington's supreme advantage lay in the fighting quality of his troops. The campaigns of six years had made them an army of veterans. "Danger," says Napier, "was their sport," and victory, it might also be added, was their habit. They fought with a confidence and fierceness which, added to the cool and stubborn courage native to the British character, made the battalions which broke over the French frontier under Wellington perhaps the most formidable fighting force known in the history of war. To quote Napier once more: "What Alexander's Macedonians were at Arbela, Hannibal's Africans at Cannae, Caesar's Romans at Pharsalia, Napoleon's Guards at Austerlitz, such were Wellington's British soldiers at this period."

On November 10, 1813, was fought what is called the battle of Nivelle, in which Wellington thrust Soult roughly and fiercely from the strong positions he held on the flanks of the great hills under which the Nivelle flows. The morning broke in great splendour; three signal-guns flashed from the heights of one of the British hills, and at once the 43rd leaped out and ran swiftly forward from the flank of the great Rhune to storm the "Hog's Back" ridge of the Petite Rhune, a ridge walled with rocks 200 feet high, except at one point, where it was protected by a marsh. William Napier, who commanded the 43rd, has told the story of the assault. He placed four companies in reserve, and led the other four in person to the attack on the rocks; and he was chiefly anxious not to rush his men—to "keep down the pace," so that they would not arrive spent and breathless at the French works. The men were eager to rush, however; the fighting impulse in them was on flame, and they were held back with difficulty. When they were still nearly 200 yards from the enemy, a youthful aide-de-camp, his blood on fire, came galloping up with a shout, and waving his hat. The 43rd broke out of hand at once with the impulse of the lad's enthusiasm and the stroke of his horse's flying hoofs, and with a sudden rush they launched themselves on the French works still high above them.

Napier had nothing for it but to join the charging mass. "I was the first man but one," he says, "who reached and jumped into the rocks, and I was only second because my strength and speed were unequal to contend with the giant who got before me. He was the tallest and most active man in the regiment, and the day before, being sentenced to corporal punishment, I had pardoned him on the occasion of an approaching action. He now repaid me by striving always to place himself between me and the fire of the enemy. His name was Eccles, an Irishman." The men won the first redoubt, but simply had not breath and strength enough left to reach the one above it, and fell gasping and exhausted in the rocks before it, the French firing fiercely upon them. In a few minutes, however, they had recovered breath; they leaped up with a shout, and tumbled over the wall of the castle; and so, from barrier to barrier, as up some Titanic stairway, the 43rd swept with glittering bayonets. The summit was held by a powerful work called the Donjon; it was so strong that attack upon it seemed madness. But a keen-eyed British officer detected signs of wavering in the French within the fort, and with a shout the 43rd leaped at it, and carried it. It took the 43rd twenty minutes to carry the whole chain of positions; and of the eleven officers of the regiment, six were killed or desperately wounded. The French showed bravery; they fought, in fact, muzzle to muzzle up the whole chain of positions. But the 43rd charged with a daring and fury absolutely resistless.

Another amazing feature in the day's fight was the manner in which Colborne, with the 52nd, carried what was called the Signal Redoubt, a strong work, crowning a steep needle-pointed hill, and overlooking the whole French position. Colborne led his men up an ascent so sharp that his horse with difficulty could climb it. The summit was reached, and the men went in, with a run, at the work, only to find the redoubt girdled by a wide ditch thirty feet deep. The men halted on the edge of the deep cutting, and under the fire of the French they fell fast. Colborne led back his men under the brow of the hill for shelter, and at three separate points brought them over the crest again. In each case, after the men had rested under shelter long enough to recover breath, the word was passed, "Stand up and advance." The men instantly obeyed, and charged up to the edge of the ditch again, many of the leading files jumping into it. But it was impossible to cross, and each time the mass of British infantry stepped coolly back into cover again.

One sergeant named Mayne, who had leaped into the ditch, found he could neither climb the ramparts nor get back to his comrades, and he flung himself on his face. A Frenchman leaned over the rampart, took leisurely aim, and fired at him as he lay. Mayne had stuck the billhook of his section at the back of his knapsack, and the bullet struck it and flattened upon it. Colborne was a man of infinite resource in war, and at this crisis he made a bugler sound a parley, hoisted his white pocket-handkerchief, and coolly walked round to the gate of the redoubt and invited the garrison to surrender. The veteran who commanded it answered indignantly, "What! I with my battalion surrender to you with yours?"

"Very well," answered Colborne in French, "the artillery will be up immediately; you cannot hold out, and you will be surrendered to the Spaniards."

That threat was sufficient. The French officers remonstrated stormily with their commander, and the work was surrendered. But only one French soldier in the redoubt had fallen, whereas amongst the 52nd "there fell," says Napier, "200 soldiers of a regiment never surpassed in arms since arms were first borne by men." In this fight Soult was driven in a little more than three hours from a mountain position he had been fortifying for more than three months.

Amongst the brave men who died that day on the side of the British were two whose portraits Napier has drawn with something of Plutarch's minuteness:

> The first, low in rank, for he was but a lieutenant; rich in honour, for he bore many scars; was young of days—he was only nineteen—and had seen more combats and sieges than he could count years. So slight in person and of such surpassing and delicate beauty that the Spaniards often thought him a girl disguised in man's clothing; he was yet so vigorous, so active, so brave, that the most daring and experienced veterans watched his looks on the field of battle, and, implicitly following where he led, would, like children, obey his slightest sign in the most difficult situations. His education was incomplete, yet were his natural

149

powers so happy that the keenest and best-furnished shrank from an encounter of wit; and every thought and aspiration was proud and noble, indicating future greatness if destiny had so willed it. Such was Edward Freer of the 43rd. The night before the battle he had that strange anticipation of coming death so often felt by military men. He was struck by three balls at the first storming of the Rhune rocks, and the sternest soldiers wept, even in the middle of the fight, when they saw him fall.

On the same day, and at the same hour, was killed Colonel Thomas Lloyd. He likewise had been a long time in the 43rd. Under him Freer had learned the rudiments of his profession; but in the course of the war, promotion placed Lloyd at the head of the 94th, and it was leading that regiment he fell. In him also were combined mental and bodily powers of no ordinary kind. Graceful symmetry, Herculean strength, and a countenance frank and majestic, gave the true index of his nature; for his capacity was great and commanding, and his military knowledge extensive, both from experience and study. Of his mirth and wit, well known in the army, it only need be said that he used the latter without offence, yet so as to increase the ascendency over those with whom he held intercourse; for, though gentle, he was ambitious, valiant, and conscious of his fitness for great exploits. And he, like Freer, was prescient of and predicted his own fall, but with no abatement of courage, for when he received the mortal wound, a most painful one, he would not suffer himself to be moved, and remained to watch the battle, mak-

ing observations upon its changes until death came. It was thus, at the age of thirty, that the good, the brave, the generous Lloyd died. Tributes to his memory have been published by Wellington, and by one of his own poor soldiers, by the highest and by the lowest. To their testimony I add mine. Let those who served on equal terms with him say whether in aught it has exaggerated his deserts.

A pathetic incident may be added, found in Napier's biography, but which he does not give in his History. The night before the battle Napier was stretched on the ground under his cloak, when young Freer came to him and crept under the cover of his cloak, sobbing as if his heart would break. Napier tried to soothe and comfort the boy, and learnt from him that he was fully persuaded he should lose his life in the approaching battle, and his distress was caused by thinking of his mother and sister in England.

On December 9, Wellington, by a daring movement and with some fierce fighting, crossed the Nive. It was a movement which had many advantages, but one drawback—his wings were now separated by the Nive; and Soult at this stage, like the great and daring commander he was, took advantage of his position to attempt a great counter-stroke. It was within his power to fling his whole force on either wing of Wellington, and so confident was he of success that he wrote to the Minister of War telling him to "expect good news" the next day. Wellington himself was on the right bank of the Nive, little dreaming that Soult was about to leap on the extremity of his scattered forces. The country was so broken that Soult's movements were entirely hidden, and the roads so bad that even the cavalry outposts could scarcely move. On the night of the

9th Soult had gathered every available bayonet, and was ready to burst on the position held by Sir John Hope at Arcanques.

In the grey dawn of the 10th the out-pickets of the 43rd noticed that the French infantry were pushing each other about as if in sport; but the crowd seemed to thicken and to eddy nearer and nearer the British line. It was a trick to deceive the vigilance of the British outposts. Presently the apparently sportive crowd made a rush forwards and re-solved itself into a spray of swiftly moving skirmishers. The French columns broke from behind a screen of houses, and, at a running pace, and with a tumult of shouts, charged the British position. In a moment the crowd of French soldiers had penetrated betwixt the 43rd and 52nd, and charging eagerly forward, tried to turn the flanks of both. But these were veteran regiments; they fell coolly and swiftly back, firing fiercely as they went. It was at once a race and a com-bat. The roads were so narrow and so bad that the British could keep no order, and if the French outpaced them and reached the open position at the rear first, the British line would be pierced. The 43rd came through the pass first, apparently a crowd of running fugitives, officers and men jumbled together. The moment they had reached the open ground, however, the men fell, as if by a single impulse, into military form, and became a steadfast red line, from end to end of which ran, and ran again, and yet again, the volleying flame of a sustained musketry fire. The pass was barred!

The troops to the right of the French were not quite so quick or so fortunate, and about 100 of the British—rifle-men and men of the 43rd—were intercepted. The French never doubted that they would surrender, for they were but a handful of men cut off by a whole column. An ensign of the 43rd named Campbell, a lad not eighteen years of age, was in the front files of the British when the call to surrender was heard. With a shout the boy-ensign leaped at the French column. Where an officer leads, British soldiers will always follow, and the men followed him with a courage as high as his own. With a rush the column was rent, and though fifty of the British were killed or taken, fifty, including the gallant boy who led them, escaped.

The fighting at other points was of the sharpest, and was strangely entangled and confused. It was a fight of infantry against infantry, and the whole field of the combat was interlaced by almost impassable hedges. At one point, so strangely broken was the ground, and so obscured the fight with smoke and mist, that a French regiment passed unseen betwixt the British and Portuguese, and was rapidly filing into line on the rear of the 9th, fiercely occupied at that moment against a strong force in front. Cameron, its colonel, left fifty men of his regiment to answer the fire in his front, faced about, and went at a run against the French regiment, which by this time had commenced volley-firing. Cameron's men fell fast—eighty men and officers, in fact, dropped in little more than five minutes—but the rush of the 9th was irresistible. The Frenchmen wavered, broke, and swept, a disorganised mass, past the flank of the Royals, actually carrying off one of its officers in the rush, and disappeared.

The sternest and most bewildering fighting took place round a building known as the "mayor's house," surrounded by a coppice-wood. Coppice and outbuildings were filled with men of all regiments and all nations, swearing, shooting, and charging with the bayonet. The 84th was caught in a hollow road by the French, who lined the banks above, and lost its colonel and a great proportion of its rank and file. Gronow tells an amusing incident of the fight at this stage. An isolated British battalion stationed near the mayor's house was suddenly surrounded by a flood of French. The French general galloped up to the British officer in command and demanded his sword. "Upon this," says Gronow, "without the least hesitation the British officer shouted out, 'This fellow wants us to surrender! Charge! my boys, and show them what stuff we are made of.'" The men answered with a shout, sudden, scornful, and stern, and went with a run at the French. "In a few minutes," adds Gronow, "they had taken prisoners or killed the whole of the infantry regiment opposed to them!"

On the 11th desperate fighting took place on the same ground, but the British were by this time reinforced—the Guards, in particular, coming up after a rapid and exhausting march—and Soult's attack had failed. But on the night of the 12th the rain fell fast and steadily, the Nive was flooded, the bridge of boats which spanned it swept away, and Hill was left at St. Pierre isolated, with less than 14,000 men. Soult saw his opportunity. The interior lines he held made concentration easy, and on the morning of the 13th he was able to pour an attacking force of 35,000 bayonets on Hill's front, while another infantry division, together with the whole of the French cavalry under Pierre Soult, attacked his rear.

CHAPTER 7

Fighting in the Passes

"In both the passes, and on the heights above them, there was desperate fighting. They fought on the mountain-tops, which could scarcely have witnessed any other combat than that of the Pyrenean eagles; they fought among jagged rocks and over profound abysses; they fought amidst clouds and mists, for those mountain-tops were 5000 feet above the level of the plain of France, and the rains, which had fallen in torrents, were evaporating in the morning and noon-day sun, were steaming heavenward and clothing the loftiest peaks with fantastic wreaths." These words describe, with picturesque force, the most brilliant and desperate, and yet, perhaps, the least known chapter in the great drama of the Peninsular war: the furious combats waged between British and French in the gloomy valleys and on the mist-shrouded summits of the Western Pyrenees. The great campaign, which found its climax at Vittoria, lasted six weeks. In that brief period Wellington marched with 100,000 men 600 miles, passed six great rivers, gained one historic and decisive battle, invested two fortresses, and drove 120,000 veteran troops from Spain. There is no more brilliant chapter in military history; and, at its close, to quote Napier's clarion-like sentences, "the English general, emerging from the chaos of the Peninsular struggle, stood on the summit of the Pyrenees a recognised conqueror. From those lofty pinnacles the clangour of his trumpets pealed clear and loud, and the splendour of his genius appeared as a flaming beacon to warring nations."

But the great barrier of the Pyrenees stretched across Wellington's path, a tangle of mountains sixty miles in length; a wild table-land rough with crags, fierce with mountain torrents, shaggy with forests, a labyrinth of savage and snow-clad hills. On either flank a great fortress—San Sebastian and Pampeluna—was held by the French, and Wellington was besieging both at once, and besieging them without battering trains. The echoes of Vittoria had aroused Napoleon, then fighting desperately on the Elbe, and ten days after Vittoria the French Emperor, acting with the lightning-like decision characteristic of his genius, had despatched Soult, the ablest of all his generals, to bar the passes of the Pyrenees against Wellington. Soult travelled day and night to the scene of his new command, gathering reinforcements on every side as he went, and in an incredibly short period he had assembled on the French side of the Pyrenees a great and perfectly equipped force of 75,000 men.

Wellington could not advance and leave San Sebastian and Pampeluna on either flank held by the enemy. Some eight separate passes pierce the giant chain of the Pyrenees. Soult was free to choose any one of them for his advance to the relief of either of the besieged fortresses, but Wellington had to keep guard over the whole eight, and the force holding each pass was almost completely isolated from its comrades. Thus all the advantages of position were with Soult. He could pour his whole force through one or two selected passes, brush aside the relatively scanty force which held it, relieve San Sebastian or Pampeluna, and, with the relieved fortress as his base, fling himself on Wellington's flank while the allied armies were scattered over the slopes of the Pyrenees for sixty miles. And Soult was exactly the general to avail himself of these advantages. He had the swift vision, the resolute will, and the daring of a great commander. "It is on Spanish soil," he said in a proclamation to his troops, "your tents must next be pitched. Let the account of our successes be dated from Vittoria, and let the fête-day of his Imperial Majesty be celebrated in that city." These were brave words, and having uttered them, Soult led his gallant troops, with gallant purpose, into the gloomy passes of the Pyrenees, and for days following the roar of battle sank and swelled over the snow-clad peaks. But when the Imperial fête-day arrived—August 15—Soult's great army was pouring back from those same passes a shattered host, and the allied troops, sternly following them, were threatening French soil!

Soult judged Pampeluna to be in greater peril than San Sebastian, and moved by his left to force the passes of Roncesvalles and Maya. The rain fell furiously, the mountain streams were in flood, gloomy mists shrouded the hill-tops; but by July 24, with more than 60,000 fighting men, and nearly seventy guns, Soult was pouring along the passes he had chosen. It is impossible to do more than pick out a few of the purple patches in the swift succession of heroic combats that followed: fights waged on mountain summits 5000 feet above the sea-level, in shaggy forests, under tempests of rain and snow. D'Erlon, with a force of 20,000 men, took the British by surprise in the pass of Maya. Ross, an eager and hardy soldier, unexpectedly encountering the French advance guard, instantly shouted the order to "Charge!"

and with a handful of the 20th flung himself upon the enemy, and actually checked their advance until Cole, who had only 10,000 bayonets to oppose to 30,000, had got into fighting form. A thick fog fell like a pall on the combatants, and checked the fight, and Cole, in the night, fell back. The French columns were in movement at daybreak, but still the fog hid the whole landscape, and the guides of the French feared to lead them up the slippery crags. At Maya, however, the French in force broke upon Stewart's division, holding that pass. The British regiments, as they came running up, not in mass, but by companies, and breathless with the run, were flung with furious haste upon the French. The 34th, the 39th, the 28th in succession crashed into the fight, but were flung back by overpowering numbers. It was a battle of 4000 men against 13,000.

The famous 50th, fiercely advancing, checked the French rush at one point; but Soult's men were full of the *élan* of victory, and swept past the British flanks. The 71st and 92nd were brought into the fight, and the latter especially clung sternly to their position till two men out of every three were shot down, the mound of dead and dying forming a solid barrier between the wasted survivors of the regiment and the shouting edge of the French advance. "The stern valour of the 92nd," says Napier, "principally composed of Irishmen, would have graced Thermopylae." No one need question the fighting quality of the Irish soldier, but, as a matter of fact, there were 825 Highlanders in the regiment, and 61 Irishmen. The British, however, were steadily pushed back, ammunition failed, and the soldiers were actually defending the highest crag with stones, when Barnes, with a brigade of the seventh division, coming breathlessly up the pass, plunged into the fight, and checked the French.

Soult had gained ten of the thirty miles of road toward Pampeluna, but at an ominous cost, and, meanwhile, the plan of his attack was developed, and Wellington was in swift movement to bar his path.

Soult had now swung into the pass of Roncesvalles, and was on the point of attacking Cole, who held the pass with a very inadequate force, when, at that exact moment, Wellington, having despatched his aides in various directions to bring up the troops, galloped alone along the mountain flank to the British line. He was recognised; the nearest troops raised a shout; it ran, gathering volume as it travelled down all the slope, where the British stood waiting for the French attack. That sudden shout, stern and exultant, reached the French lines, and they halted. At the same moment, round the shoulder of the hill on the opposite side of the pass, Soult appeared, and the two generals, near enough to see each other's features, eagerly scrutinised one another. "Yonder is a great commander," said Wellington, as if speaking to himself, "but he is cautious, and will delay his attack to ascertain the cause of these cheers. That will give time for the sixth division to arrive, and I shall beat him." Wellington's forecast of Soult's action was curiously accurate. He made no attack that day. The sixth division came up, and Soult was beaten!

There were two combats of Sauroren, and each was, in Wellington's own phrase, "bludgeon work"—a battle of soldiers rather than of generals, a tangle of fierce charges and counter-charges, of volleys delivered so close that they scorched the very clothes of the opposing lines, and sustained so fiercely that they died down only because the lines of desperately firing men crumbled into ruin and silence. Nothing could be finer than the way in which a French

column, swiftly, sternly, and without firing a shot, swept up
a craggy steep crowned by rocks like castles, held by some
Portuguese battalions, and won the position. Ross's brigade,
in return, with equal vehemence recharged the position
from its side, and dashed the French out of it; the French in
still greater force came back, a shouting mass, and crushed
Ross's men. Then Wellington sent forward Byng's brigade
at running pace, and hurled the French down the mountain
side. At another point in the pass the French renewed their
assault four times; in their second assault they gained the
summit. The 40th were in reserve at that point; they waited
in steady silence till the edge of the French line, a confused
mass of tossing bayonets and perspiring faces, came clear
over the crest; then, running forward with extraordinary
fury, they flung them, a broken, tumultuous mass, down
the slope. In the later charges, so fierce and resolute were
the French officers that they were seen dragging their tired
soldiers up the hill by their belts!

It is idle to attempt the tale of this wild mountain fighting. Soult at last fell back, and Wellington followed, swift
and vehement, on his track, and moved Alten's column to
intercept the French retreat. The story of Alten's march
is a marvellous record of soldierly endurance. His men
pressed on with speed for nineteen consecutive hours, and
covered forty miles of mountain tracks, wilder than the
Otway Ranges, or the paths of the Austrian Alps between
Bright and Omeo. The weather was close; many men fell
and died, convulsed and frothing at the mouth. Still, their
officers leading, the regiment kept up its quick step, till,
as evening fell, the head of the column reached the edge
of the precipice overlooking the bridge across which, in
all the confusion of a hurried retreat, the French troops

were crowding. "We overlooked the enemy," says Cook in his *Memoirs*, "at stone's-throw. The river separated us; but the French were wedged in a narrow road, with inaccessible rocks on one side, and the river on the other." Who can describe the scene that followed! Some of the French fired vertically up at the British; others ran; others shouted for quarter; some pointed with eager gestures to the wounded, whom they carried on branches of trees, as if entreating the British not to fire.

In nine days of continual marching, ten desperate actions had been fought, at what cost of life can hardly be reckoned. Napier, after roughly calculating the losses, says: "Let this suffice. It is not needful to sound the stream of blood in all its horrid depths." But the fighting sowed the wild passes of the Pyrenees thick with the graves of brave men.

Soult actually fought his way to within sight of the walls of Pampeluna, and its beleaguered garrison waved frantic welcomes to his columns as, from the flanks of the overshadowing hills, they looked down on the city. Then broken as by the stroke of a thunderbolt, and driven like wild birds caught in a tempest, the French poured back through the passes to French soil again. "I never saw such fighting," was Wellington's comment on the struggle.

For the weeks that followed, Soult could only look on while San Sebastian and Pampeluna fell. Then the allied outposts were advanced to the slopes looking down on France and the distant sea. It is recorded that the Highlanders of Hill's division, like Xenophon's Greeks 2000 years before them, broke into cheers when they caught their first glimpse of the sea, the great, wrinkled, azure-tinted floor, flecked with white sails. It was "the way home!" Bearn and Gascony and Languedoc lay stretched like a map under their feet. But the weather was bitter, the snow lay thick in the passes, sentinels were frozen at the outposts, and a curious stream of desertions began. The warm plains of sunny France tempted the half-frozen troops, and Southey computes, with an arithmetical precision which is half-humorous, that the average weekly proportion of desertions was 25 Spaniards, 15 Irish, 12 English, 6 Scotch, and half a Portuguese! One indignant English colonel drew up his regiment on parade, and told the men that "if any of them wanted to join the French they had better do so at once. He gave them free leave. He wouldn't have men in the regiment who wished to join the enemy!"

Meanwhile Soult was trying to construct on French soil lines of defence as mighty as those of Wellington at Torres Vedras; and on October 7, Wellington pushed his left across the Bidassoa, the stream that marks the boundaries of Spain and France. On the French side the hills rise to a great height. One huge shoulder, called La Rhune, commands the whole stream; another lofty ridge, called the "Boar's Back," offered almost equal facilities for defence. The only road that crossed the hills rose steeply, with sharp zigzags, and for weeks the French had toiled to make the whole position impregnable. The British soldiers had watched while the mountain sides were scarred with trenches, and the road was blocked with abattis, and redoubt rose above redoubt like a gigantic staircase climbing the sky. The Bidassoa at its mouth is wide, and the tides rose sixteen feet.

But on the night of October 7—a night wild with rain and sleet—Wellington's troops marched silently to their assigned posts on the banks of the river. When day broke, at a signal-gun seven columns could be seen moving at once in a line of five miles, and before Soult could detect Wellington's plan the river was crossed, the French entrenched camps on the Bidassoa won! The next morning the heights were attacked. The Rifles carried the Boar's Back with a single effort. The Bayonette Crest, a huge spur guarded by battery above battery, and crowned by a great redoubt, was attacked by Colborne's brigade and some Portuguese. The tale of how the hill was climbed, and the batteries carried in swift succession, cannot be told here. It was a warlike feat of the most splendid quality. Other columns moving along the flanks of the great hill alarmed the French lest they should be cut off, and they abandoned the redoubt on the summit. Colborne, accompanied by only one of his staff and half-a-dozen files of riflemen, came suddenly round a shoulder of the hill on the whole garrison of the redoubt, 300 strong, in retreat. With great presence of mind, he ordered them, in the sharpest tones of authority, to "lay down their arms," and, believing themselves cut off, they obeyed!

A column of Spanish troops moving up the flanks of the great Rhune found their way barred by a strong line of abattis and the fire of two French regiments. The column halted, and their officers vainly strove to get the Spaniards to attack. An officer of the 43rd named Havelock—a name yet more famous in later wars—attached to Alten's staff, was sent to see what caused the stoppage of the column. He found the Spaniards checked by the great abattis, through which flashed, fierce and fast, the fire of the French. Waving his hat, he shouted to the Spaniards to "follow him," and, putting his horse at the abattis, at one leap went headlong amongst the French. There is a swift contagion in valour. He was only a light-haired lad, and the Spaniards with one vehement shout for "*el chico blanco*"—"the fair lad"—swept over abattis and French together!

CHAPTER 8

Orthez

Hill's front stretched through two miles; his left; a wooded craggy ridge, was held by Pringle's brigade, but was parted from the centre by a marshy valley and a chain of ponds; his centre occupied a crescent-shaped broken ridge; his right, under General Byng, held a ridge parallel with the Adour. The French gathered in great masses on a range of counter-heights, an open plain being between them and Hill's centre. The day was heavy with whirling mist; and as the wind tore it occasionally asunder, the British could see on the parallel roads before them the huge, steadily flowing columns of the French.

Abbé led the attack on the British centre. He was "the fighting general" of Soult's army, famous for the rough energy of his character and the fierceness of his onfall. He pushed his attack with such ardour that he forced his way to the crest of the British ridge. The famous 92nd, held in reserve, was brought forward by way of counter-stroke, and pushed its attack keenly home. The head of Abbé's column was crushed; but the French general replaced the broken battalions by fresh troops, and still forced his way onward, the 92nd falling back.

In the meanwhile on both the right and the left of the British position an almost unique disaster had befallen Hill's

troops. Peacock, the colonel of the 71st, through some be-
witched failure of nerve or of judgment, withdrew that
regiment from the fight. It was a Highland regiment, great
in fighting reputation, and full of daring. How black were
the looks of the officers, and what loud swearing in Gaelic
took place in the ranks, as the gallant regiment—discipline
overcoming human nature—obeyed the mysterious order
to retire, may be imagined. Almost at the same moment on
the right, Bunbury, who commanded the 3rd or Buffs, in
the same mysterious fashion abandoned to the French the
strong position he held. Both colonels were brave men, and
their sudden lapse into unsoldierly conduct has never been
explained. Both, it may be added, were compelled to resign
their commissions after the fight.

Hill, surveying the spectacle from the post he had taken,
commanding the whole field of battle, hastened down, met
and halted the Buffs, sent them back to the fight, drew his
whole reserves into the fray, and himself turned the 71st
and led them to the attack. With what joy the indignant
Highlanders of the 71st obeyed the order to "Right about
face" may be imagined, and so vehement was their charge
that the French column upon which it was flung, though
coming on at the double, in all the *élan* of victory, was instantly shattered.

Meanwhile the 92nd was launched again at Abbé's column. Cameron, its colonel, was a soldier of a very gallant
type, and, himself a Highlander, he understood the Highland temperament perfectly. He dressed his regiment as
if on parade, the colours were uncased, the pipes shrilled
fiercely, and in all the pomp of military array, with green
tartans and black plumes all wind-blown, and with the
wild strains of their native hills and lochs thrilling in their

ears, the Highlanders bore down on the French, their officers fiercely leading. On all sides at that moment the British skirmishers were falling back. The 50th was clinging desperately to a small wood that crowned the ridge, but everywhere the French were forcing their way onward. Ashworth's Portuguese were practically destroyed; Barnes, who commanded the centre, was shot through the body. But the fierce charge of the 92nd along the high-road, and of the 71st on the left centre, sent an electric thrill along the whole British front. The skirmishers, instead of falling back, ran forward; the Portuguese rallied. The 92nd found in its immediate front two strong French regiments, and their leading files brought their bayonets to the charge, and seemed eager to meet the 92nd with the actual push of steel. It was the crisis of the fight.

At that moment the French commander's nerve failed him. That steel-edged line of kilted, plume-crested Highlanders, charging with a step so fierce, was too much for him. He suddenly turned his horse, waved his sword; his men promptly faced about, and marched back to their original position. The French on both the right and the left drew back, and the battle for the moment seemed to die down. Hill's right was safe, and he drew the 57th from it to strengthen his sorely battered centre; and just at that moment the sixth division, which had been marching since daybreak, crossed the bridge over the Nive, which the British engineers with rare energy had restored, and appeared on the ridge overlooking the field of battle. Wellington, too, appeared on the scene, with the third and fourth divisions. At two o'clock the allies commenced a forward movement, and Soult fell back; his second counter-stroke had failed.

St. Pierre was, perhaps, the most desperately contested fight in the Peninsular war, a field almost as bloody as Albuera. Hill's ranks were wasted as by fire; three British generals were carried from the field; nearly the whole of the staff was struck down. On a space scarcely one mile square, 5000 men were killed and wounded within three hours. Wellington, as he rode over the field by the side of Hill after the fight was over, declared he had never seen the dead lie so thickly before. It was a great feat for less than 14,000 men with 14 guns to withstand the assault of 35,000 men with 22 guns; and, at least where Abbé led, the fighting of the French was of the most resolute character. The victory was due, in part, to Hill's generalship and the lion-like energy with which he restored his broken centre and flung back the Buffs and the 71st into the fight. But in a quite equal degree the victory was due to the obstinate fighting quality of the British private. The 92nd, for example, broke the French front no less than four times by bayonet charges pushed home with the sternest resolution, and it lost in these charges 13 officers and 171 rank and file.

The French, it might almost be said, lost the field by the momentary failure in nerve of the officer commanding the column upon which the 92nd was rushing in its last and most dramatic charge. His column was massive and unbroken; the men, with bent heads and levelled bayonets, were ready to meet the 92nd with a courage as lofty as that of the Highlanders themselves, and the 92nd, for all its parade of fluttering colours and wind-blown tartans and feathers, was but a single weak battalion. An electrical gesture, a single peremptory call on the part of the leader, even a single daring act by a soldier in the ranks, and the French column would have been hurled on the 92nd, and by its mere weight must have broken it. But the oncoming of the Highlanders proved too great a strain for the nerve of the French general. He wheeled the head of his horse backward, and the fight was lost.

Weeks of the bitterest winter weather suspended all military operations after St. Pierre. The rivers were flooded; the clayey lowlands were one far-stretching quagmire; fogs brooded in the ravines; perpetual tempests shrieked over the frozen summits of the Pyrenees; the iron-bound coast was furious with breakers. But Wellington's hardy veterans—ill-clad, ill-sheltered, and ill-fed—yet kept their watch on the slopes of the Pyrenees. The outposts of the two armies, indeed, fell into almost friendly relations with each other. Barter sprang up between them, a regular code of signals was established, friendly offices were exchanged. Wellington on one occasion desired to reconnoitre Soult's camp from the top of a hill occupied by a French picket, and ordered some English rifles to drive them off. No firing was necessary. An English soldier held up the butt of his rifle and tapped it in a peculiar way. The signal meant, "We must have the hill for a short time," and the French at once retired. A steady traffic in brandy and tobacco sprang up between the pickets of the two armies. A rivulet at one point flowed between the outposts, and an Irish soldier named Patten, on sentry there, placed a canteen with a silver coin in it on a stone by the bank of the rivulet, to be filled with brandy by the French in the usual way. Canteen and coin vanished, but no brandy arrived. Patten, a daring fellow, regarded himself as cheated, and the next day seeing, as he supposed, the same French sentry on duty, he crossed the rivulet, seized the Frenchman's musket, shook the amazed sentry out of his accoutrements as a pea is shaken out of its pod, and carried them off. The French outposts sent in a flag of truce, complained of this treatment, and said the unfortunate sentry's life would be forfeited unless his uniform and gun were restored. Patten, however, insisted that he held these "in pawn for a canteen of brandy," and he got his canteen before the uniform was restored.

On February 12 a white hard frost suddenly fell on the whole field of operations, and turned the viscid mud everywhere to the hardness of stone. The men could march, the artillery move; and Wellington, whose strategy was ripe, was at once in action.

Soult barred his path by a great entrenched camp at Bayonne, to which the Adour served as a Titanic wet ditch. The Adour is a great river, swift and broad—swiftest and broadest through the six miles of its course below the town to its mouth. Its bed is of shifting sand; the spring-tide rises in it fourteen feet, the ebb-tide runs seven miles an hour. Where the swift river and the great rollers of the Bay of Biscay meet is a treacherous bar—in heavy weather a mere tumult of leaping foam. Soult assumed that Wellington would cross the river above the town; the attempt to cross it near the mouth, where it was barred with sand, and beaten with surges, and guarded, too, by a tiny squadron of French gunboats, was never suspected. Yet exactly this was Wellington's plan; and his bridge across the Adour is declared by Napier to be a stupendous undertaking, which must always rank amongst "the prodigies of war." Forty large sailing-boats, of about twenty tons burden each, carrying the materials for the bridge, were to enter the mouth of the Adour at the moment when Hope, with part of

Hill's division, made his appearance on the left bank of the river, with materials for rafts, by means of which sufficient troops could be thrown across the Adour to capture a battery which commanded its entrance.

On the night of February 22, Hope, with the first division, was in the assigned position on the banks of the Adour, hidden behind some sandhills. But a furious gale made the bar impassable, and not a boat was in sight. Hope, the most daring of men, never hesitated; he would cross the river without the aid of the fleet. His guns were suddenly uncovered, the tiny French flotilla was sunk or scattered, and a pontoon or raft, carrying sixty men of the Guards, pushed out from the British bank. A strong French picket held the other shore; but, bewildered and ill led, they made no opposition. A hawser was dragged across the stream, and pontoons, each carrying fifteen men, were in quick succession pulled across. When about a thousand men had in this way reached the French bank, some French battalions made their appearance. Colonel Stopford, who was in command, allowed the French to come on—their drums beating the *pas de charge*, and their officers waving their swords—to within a distance of twenty yards, and then opened upon them with his rocket brigade. The fiery flight and terrifying sound of these missiles put the French to instant rout. All night the British continued to cross, and on the morning of the 24th the flotilla was off the bar, the boats of the men-of-war leading.

The first boat that plunged into the tumult of breakers, leaping and roaring over the bar, sank instantly. The second shot through and was safe; but the tide was running out furiously, and no boat could follow till it was high water again. When high water came, the troops crowding the sandbanks watched with breathless interest the fight of the boats to enter. They hung and swayed like a flock of gigantic sea-birds on the rough and tumbling sea. Lieutenant Bloye of the *Lyra*, who led the way in his barge, dashed into the broad zone of foam, and was instantly swallowed up with all his crew. The rest of the flotilla bore up to right and left, and hovered on the edge of the tormented waters. Suddenly Lieutenant Cheyne of the *Woodlark* caught a glimpse of the true course and dashed through, and boat after boat came following with reeling decks and dripping crews; but in the whole passage no fewer than eight of the flotilla were destroyed. The bridge was quickly constructed. Thirty-six two-masted vessels were moored head to stern, with an interval between each vessel, across the 800 yards of the Adour; a double line of cables, about ten feet apart, linked the boats together; strong planks were lashed athwart the cables, making a roadway; a double line of masts, forming a series of floating squares, served as a floating boom; and across this swaying, flexible, yet mighty bridge, Wellington was able to pour his left wing, with all its artillery and material, and so draw round Bayonne an iron line of investment.

This movement thrust back Soult's right, but he clung obstinately to the Gave. He held by Napoleon's maxim that the best way to defend is to attack, and Wellington's very success gave him what seemed a golden opportunity. Wellington's left had crossed the Adour, but that very movement separated it from the right.

Soult took up his position on a ridge of hills above Orthez. He commanded the fords by which Picton must cross, and his plan was to crush him while in the act of crossing. The opportunity was clear, but somehow Soult missed it. There failed him at the critical moment the swift-attacking impulse which both Napoleon and Wellington possessed in so high a degree. Picton's two divisions crossed the Gave, and climbed the bank through mere fissures in the rocks, which broke up all military order, and the nearest point which allowed them to fall into line was within cannon-shot of the enemy. Even Picton's iron nerve shook at such a crisis; but Wellington, to use Napier's phrase, "calm as deepest sea," watched the scene. Soult ought to have attacked; he waited to be attacked, and so missed victory.

By nine o'clock Wellington had formed his plan, and Ross's brigade was thrust through a gorge on Soult's left. The French were admirably posted: they had a narrow front, abundant artillery, and a great battery placed so as to smite on the flank any column forcing its way through the gorge which pierced Soult's left. Ross's men fought magnificently. Five times they broke through the gorge, and five times the fire of the French infantry on the slopes above them, and the grape of the great battery at the head of the gorge, drove the shattered regiments back. On Soult's right, again, Foy flung back with loss an attack by part of Picton's forces. On both the right and left, that is, Soult was victorious, and, as he saw the wasted British lines roll sullenly back, it is said that the French general smote his thigh in exultation, and cried, "At last I have him!"

Almost at that moment, however, the warlike genius of Wellington changed the aspect of the scene. He fed the attacks on Soult's right and left, and the deepening roar of the battle at these two points absorbed the senses of the French general. Soult's front was barred by what was supposed to be an impassable marsh, above which a

great hill frowned; and across the marsh, and upon this hill, the centre of Soult's position, Wellington launched the famous 52nd.

Colborne plunged with his men into the marsh; they sank at every step above the knee, sometimes to the middle. The skirmishers shot fiercely at them. But with stern composure the veterans of the light division—soldiers, as Napier never tires in declaring, who "had never yet met their match in the field"—pressed on. The marsh was crossed, the hill climbed, and with a sudden and deafening shout—the cheer which has a more full and terrible note than any other voice of fighting men, the shout of the British regiment as it charges—the 52nd dashed between Foy and Taupin. A French battalion in their path was scattered as by the stroke of a thunderbolt. The French centre was pierced; both victorious wings halted, and began to ebb back. Hill, meanwhile, had crossed the Gave, and taking a wider circle, threatened Soult's line of retreat. The French fell back, and fell back with ever-quickening steps, but yet fighting sternly; the British, with deafening musketry and cannonade, pressed on them. Hill quickened his pace on the ridge along which he was pressing. It became a race who should reach first the single bridge on the Luy-de-Béarn over which the French must pass. The pace became a run. Many of the French broke from their ranks and raced forward. The British cavalry broke through some covering battalions and sabred the fugitives. A great disaster was imminent; and yet it was avoided, partly by Soult's cool and obstinate defence, and partly by the accident that at that moment Wellington was struck by a spent ball and was disabled, so that his swift and imperious will no longer directed the pursuit.

Orthez may be described as the last and not the least glorious fight in the Peninsular war. Toulouse was fought ten day afterwards, but it scarcely belongs to the Peninsular campaigns, and was actually fought after a general armistice had been signed.

ALSO FROM LEONAUR

AVAILABLE IN SOFTCOVER OR HARDCOVER WITH DUST JACKET

EW2 EYEWITNESS TO WAR SERIES
CAPTAIN OF THE 95th (Rifles) *by Jonathan Leach*

An officer of Wellington's Sharpshooters during the
Peninsular, South of France and Waterloo Campaigns
of the Napoleonic Wars.

SOFTCOVER : **ISBN 1-84677-001-7**
HARDCOVER : **ISBN 1-84677-016-5**

WF1 THE WARFARE FICTION SERIES
NAPOLEONIC WAR STORIES
by Sir Arthur Quiller-Couch

Tales of soldiers, spies, battles & Sieges from the
Peninsular & Waterloo campaigns

SOFTCOVER : **ISBN 1-84677-003-3**
HARDCOVER : **ISBN 1-84677-014-9**

EW1 EYEWITNESS TO WAR SERIES
RIFLEMAN COSTELLO *by Edward Costello*

The adventures of a soldier of the 95th (Rifles) in the
Peninsular & Waterloo Campaigns of the Napoleonic wars.

SOFTCOVER : **ISBN 1-84677-000-9**
HARDCOVER : **ISBN 1-84677-018-1**

MC1 THE MILITARY COMMANDERS SERIES
JOURNALS OF ROBERT ROGERS OF THE RANGERS *by Robert Rogers*

The exploits of Rogers & the Rangers in his own words
during 1755-1761 in the French & Indian War.

SOFTCOVER : **ISBN 1-84677-002-5**
HARDCOVER : **ISBN 1-84677-010-6**

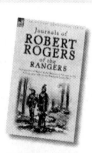

Printed in the United Kingdom
by Lightning Source UK Ltd.
123162UK00001BA/67-69/A